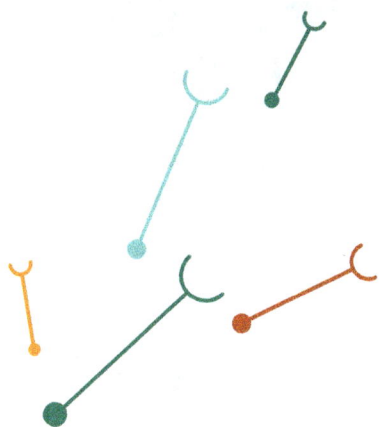

everything breathes

ryan miller

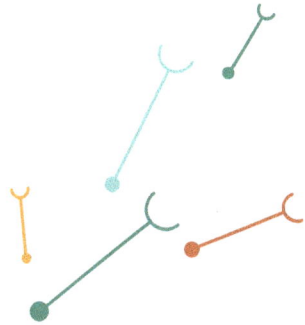

To the backers.

You are the encouragers, the supporters, and the friends.

Your stories and your trust is what fuels the fire.

(listed chronologically)

the fowlers
Jessica and Matthew Roy
Kris Mayhew
Heather Brandt
Crecelii
Manny Trembley
John & Susy Breneman
Rand and Robin Miller
Valentine Family
Steven Cutter
Josh Staub
Kyle & Kay C. England
Jeff Näslund
Anonymous
Rob and Megan Kennedy
Dan Downing
John Burris

The Tang Family: David, Corey, Darian and Miara
Karli Ingersoll
Mom and Dad
Brice Tebbs
Dad and Mom Leaf
Paula Ordway
Christopher Webber
Dan and Lisa Leaf
Christopher Johnson
Brandon & Abbey Campea
Dana Brightman
Asia and Cathy Goins
Cathy and Colleen Fagan
Jim and Michelle Hereford
Nancy Janzen
Bryan "B.D." Dormaier
Andrew "Deg" Chernauskas
Tyler & Kelly Lafferty
Jeff and Jenny Oswalt
Mary Lynn Eberle
Scott and Eleri Hamilton
Meredith
Sir Jesse Sean MacDonald I
James and Stacy Hill
Sean Tyson
anonymous
James Collas
Julia Johnsen
MCCOLLOUGH FAMILY
Whitney & Jordan Tampien
Darcy, Aaron, Keagan, Kinkade, Lucia and Emery
Emily Mikkelsen
Her Royal Highness Jamie Fiorino
Tiffany and Nathan Gonzalez
Kathy Taylor
Brian Jamieson
Natalie Blashill
Barbara Buley
Jordan Baker
Tara Civitillo
Melanie Walters
The Gilbert Family

Anonymous
Kari Cardon
Nicholas Kemner
anonymous
Donald Brown
kpl and ggl
Joe and Angie Feryn
Devon Strang
Alain 'Meta' Guignard
Thomas and Kirsten
Jonathan and Michele Pasma
Chris Doyle
Kyle Nash
Josh
Aimee
Troy and Karri Clute
Steve Hoogendyk
Dear sweet awesome auntie!
Jen Gockley
Sheli Williams
Ryan Warzecha
anonymous
Jeff Lanctot
Lord and Lady Edwards
Jason Calvert
Robyn Miller & Mischa Jakupcak
Emily McBroom
Pat and Patty
gabe and missi mccloskey
Heavenly Trum
Matt and Tricia Kinder
Dave Hannon
anonymous
Donna Kendall
Luke & Jordyn Hopkins
Dave and Courtney Smith
Ian Panzer
Shanny
Gayle and Barry Husfloen
Eric
eaa
The Naslund Family

Kent and Linda
anonymous
Dan and Dawn Lenz
Katie Postma
anonymous
Tina Lynn Hickman
Brandy & Tom Steen
Jaybone
Lucy Cali
Tyler Whitney
Kevin Anderson Wilson
Nate Metheny
Matt & Meaghan Beever
Brad and Julie Jones
Chuck B

And to the four ultimate backers.

They define the word.
They support in every way possible.
With every part of their being.

Heidi, Isaac, Abbey, and Anna

Love you.

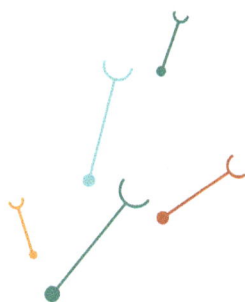

one

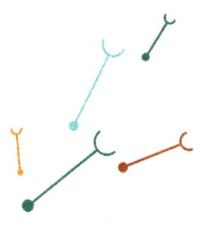

caribou

My family and I were out riding our bikes on a Sunday afternoon. It was one of those Sunday afternoons that Sunday afternoons are supposed to be: blue skies, warm air, laughs, relaxation, rest, and fun. It was almost perfect. The weather hadn't been great and it was finally time for everyone to get outside and enjoy life. And breathe.

My family consists of my wife, two teenagers, an eight-year-old and me. We were all riding on a paved trail that ran alongside a newly constructed freeway. The trail is called *Children of the Sun* because the name in the Salish language is tied to the name of our city, Spokane. On that day we all felt like children of the sun—or children of Spokane, for that matter.

Until *he* came along. You know *that* guy. He was wearing a cycling jersey and riding alone at what he thought was a very fast speed. I'm sure he was training for the Tour de France on the family-friendly trail, and our family was not what he wanted getting in his way.

As he passed by my wife and eight-year-old, he said, "Hey, if you're going to ride on the trail, you've got to stay on the right side." My wife responded—I had stopped and was taking pictures with my son—very politely: "I'm sorry. We were just having fun, enjoying the day. Sorry." To which he said, "Ride on the right or don't ride."

At that point, my daughter veered a little into the center of the trail, oblivious to the next Lance Armstrong who was meandering his way past us—obviously not at his full training speed. And that's when he yelled out, "See! Because of stuff like that!"

I wasn't quite sure what the "stuff like that" was. He had moved and easily missed my daughter.

At that point, my wife said, "Have a nice day!" He replied with a loud "You, too, dumbass!"

Dumbass? My wife or the eight-year-old with pigtails?

My wife inquired, "Why don't you try enjoying life for a second?" He responded with another mumble of "ass" as he raced away.

I thought about chasing him and accidentally bumping his tire or asking him which race he was training for, or saying something like "I didn't know they made cycling jerseys that large!" And then I realized that I was no longer enjoying the day either. Self-fulfilling I suppose. Just call my wife or daughter a dumbass and I will probably turn into one pretty quickly before I realize that's not what I want to be.

I had to wait five minutes before I could enjoy that perfect day again because I was so consumed with why the guy in the cycling jersey wasn't enjoying *it* himself. Worse, why did he have to spread his crap to us?

My family and I were driving from Spokane to Seattle. On the way is a lovely, little town called Ellensburg. One negative with Ellensburg is that it usually smells like cow manure because of the surrounding cattle ranches. On the plus side, Ellensburg rests at the bottom of the Cascade Mountains and is a great spot to stop, grab a burger, and fill up the tank.

It was Memorial Day weekend, and everyone was there for the same reason. The line for Wendy's was thirty minutes. We looked up restaurants on the iPhone and found a taco stand with rave reviews. I dropped off the family and filled up our truck across the street. I didn't realize it was ten cents more a gallon, but I should have when the attendant came to my window and told me that he would fill it up and that I couldn't.

Then he started talking to me as he filled up my truck with me sitting in the driver's seat watching him. (This, by the way, is not a job that makes much sense to me. I thought this often as I watched him doing something I've done a thousand times.) Soon (it doesn't take long to fill up a truck) the conversation got around to the owner of the gas station. The owner was in the hospital and apparently "about ready to croak". At least that's what the guy filling up my truck told me.

He then went on to say how much money the owner makes, how the owner won't put any money into the gas station or the associated car wash to make them better, how all the employees really don't like the owner because he pays everyone really poorly, and how—at the end of the day—if the owner were to die, no one would really care that much. No parades here.

We had to wait thirty minutes for our pork tacos (which were great). While I sat there in the plastic chair watching the cars drive by and staring at the gas station (which looked like something built in the communist era in Eastern Europe), I thought about that owner. What a way to go . . . with all your employees hardly able to contain themselves from talking to complete strangers about you. Like *that*.

Our family sat down to watch the premiere of *North America*, brought to us by the same people who brought us *Planet Earth*. If something is brought to us by those "same people," we'll watch it.

Tom Selleck (a.k.a. Magnum, P.I.) was soon telling us about the roaming herds of caribou in the northern-most sections of North America. The herds are so large that they have to constantly keep moving or the thousands of caribou will starve for lack of grasses on the terrain. At one point—as we watched a newborn come onto the scene among the many adults—Mr. Selleck said, "Born into a life of perpetual motion, this newborn had to run within hours to keep pace."

My wife and I both looked at each other. I was suddenly not sure whether we were watching a show about caribou in Labrador, Canada, or about human beings in Spokane—and every other city I know.

There are stories like this all day, every day. I don't know if you see or hear them, but I do all the time.

What's happening?
What's going on?
What's the problem?
What's wrong with all of us?
Where is this world going?

These are the kinds of questions that we throw around with friends when something horrible happens. They're also the kind of questions that are usually brought up when parents begin talking about youth sports.

And these are the kinds of questions that I'm often asked, in one form or another, because I'm a pastor. Somehow, someone came up with the idea that pastors are supposed to have answers to these questions. If I could meet this someone, I would have some words for him or her.

But maybe that's just *my* problem because I never wanted to be a pastor.

I did have a deal with God, though: if God wanted me to be a pastor, God would have to make it without-a-doubt obvious and clear. If God did *that*, I would fulfill my end of the bargain and do it. But I meant *clear*. Burning bush-type stuff. (And if that burning bush in the Bible wasn't literal, well I wanted a literal one.)

I didn't want to go to Bible school or seminary or even get a theology degree, and I definitely didn't want to try to start a church. None of those felt like a good fit for me and my personality. Fortunately, without any of those options, it was going to be pretty hard to become a pastor, which was all very fine with me. It's hard to have a burning bush if you don't even have a bush to light on fire.

After making the deal, or at least convincing myself that I would never be a pastor, I made video games. I spent ten years working for a game company and it was good, creative work. I got the chance to contribute to books, write scripts, imagine thousands of years of history for entire civilizations, and envision new worlds with creatures and plants and weather patterns. I also got to design puzzles and quests to make it even more entertaining.

While making video games, I started a card company with my wife. We created holiday cards, birthday cards, wedding invitations, and cards for every occasion. Another creative outlet.

Things were rolling along according to plan.

Then the unthinkable happened and a church offered me a job.[1] The church was losing a number of part-time staff, and it turned out that much of my expertise with graphic design, website administration, mentoring college students, and (apparently) speaking could fill those roles.

A friend told me I *had* to take the job. He was right. Why would a church offer me a job with no training and no experience? They wouldn't—at least that's what I thought.

The deal was on. It wasn't a *literal* burning bush, but close enough.

As things would have it, I was thrown into the deep end of the pastor pool and told to start swimming. Maybe it was a pastor ocean. I gave a sermon (one of my first-ever) my first day on the job—literally, my first official day at nine in the morning.

My first year of being a pastor was like most first years of doing new things. You look back after you've done it for awhile and cringe a little. I didn't necessarily cringe at the work I did; I expected there would be growing pains in learning the craft. I cringed because I still didn't know who I was or what I was saying. I didn't have a voice. If someone asked me, "What do you have to say?" my answers would have been pretty cliché and empty. I had all the standard "Christian" answers down perfectly.

Looking back, I don't think I had a voice because I don't think I was very sure of Christianity in general. To be honest, I found much of the standard line of thinking to be pretty boring, apathetic, and just plain ignorant at times. Even worse, there wasn't a lot of room to play, or experiment, with different answers to different questions because everyone had everything pretty well figured out. If people found different answers, well, those were "wrong" because they "weren't Christian" and, well . . . you get stuck pretty fast. I remember a pastor telling me that I could not believe in evolution and be a Christian at the same time.

What?

Yet, there was something meaningful and beautiful in my faith as well. I couldn't give it *all* up. I didn't want to. So I kept looking around for people with different answers or ways of thinking. It turns out there are thousands and thousands of people who feel, and have felt, the same way. (Who knew?) Many had felt the same way for years—arguably since the inception of this whole "Christian" thing. These people had written books, given sermons, and held conferences. It turned out there were more versions and varieties of the Christian thing than the few I had heard, and many of them were much older—and more original—than the one I had thought was the only one with all the right answers. Talk about refreshing.

In the summer of 2009 it all started to come together. I attended a conference, of sorts, on preaching. Something happened. Things began to click, not in my head, but in my heart. I hung out with some new friends. That was huge. I read more books. That helped. But, more than anything, I think I was ready to be inspired and moved and changed. I actually found something beautiful about church, about God, and about Christianity again.

I started to breathe again.

I had passion. I had something to say, and it was liberating and optimistic and my whole view of the world began to change. I had been a pretty cynical, sarcastic person who also happened to think I knew everything. (I wasn't that different than most of my Christian friends.) I called myself a realist because all pessimists do, but once you're an optimist, you realize that's just a front. I can admit that now. Or maybe I can admit it because I more fully understand it now.

Richard Rohr writes that all true Christians are optimists, and that "if you are not an optimist, you haven't got it yet."[2] Not sure if that's everyone's story, but it sure was mine and I would agree.

Christianity is a *world* of optimism. Talk about refreshing.

My perspective went from pointing out how pathetic and depressing everything and everyone is, to pointing out how exhilarating and exciting things are—even within the tragedies of life—and how much better we and society and culture can be. I went from believing it was my job to remind people that God was angry to reminding them that God was madly in love. No matter what. I went from believing that humans were pathetic, little, sinful peasants bowing to a God-King who could barely stand us, to believing that humans could change the world and that a loving empowering God wanted us to—and maybe is even waiting for us to.

People came up to me that summer and said that something had changed, and whatever it was, they liked it.

I liked it too.

There had always been talk about potentially starting a new church. Six months after that "summer of change," I found my wife crying one Sunday morning. She told me that God told her we were starting a church. Not that we *should*, but that we *were* going to.

My wife had never said anything like that before. If you know my wife, you know she's not one to say things like "God told me . . ." And if you know me, you know I get really nervous when someone says "God told me . . ." But, this time, something seemed right in the deepest parts of my being. I *knew* she was right.

Not a literal burning bush, but . . .

In 2010 we started a church called Branches. We started it in the building where I used to make video games. My former office became a nursery on the first Sunday of service. The tagline of the first video game I worked on was "The surrealistic adventure that will become your world."

I was now living that adventure, and it was, in fact, very surreal.

That thing that started in me *that* summer was really allowed to run free and take on its own life at Branches. We started with four words: simple (not indulgent), safe (for anyone), giving (money and church should not be friends), and risky (not afraid to try new things and fail).

It's been almost three years now, and they have been some of the greatest three years of my life. I'm in love with Branches.

Oliver Wendell Holmes provided the famous quote: "I would not give a fig for the simplicity this side of complexity, but I would give my life for the simplicity on the other side of complexity." In other words, when we hear an eighth-grader say, "I love her!" about his secret crush, we all smile patronizingly. When we hear an eighty-five-year-old man say that about a partner whom he's been with for sixty-five-plus years, we feel like our soul has just been rocked by the blast from a jet engine.

When I say I'm in love with Branches, I'm somewhere in-between those two examples; we've been through some things, and I'm falling hard for her.

I now *know* the church is beautiful. I might have believed it three years ago when we started, or at least hoped it, but I've seen it and felt it in a variety of ways now.

I now *know* that people are amazing and powerful. I might have believed it three years ago, or at least hoped it, but I've seen individuals give themselves for others. I've seen them welcome strangers, and I've seen them transform and grow and comfort and cry and laugh.

I still get to do fun, creative work. I write, imagine, envision, design, speak, and meet all kinds of people. In meeting people, I hear lots of stories. In hearing lots of stories, I hear lots of answers. And then, eventually, I'm expected to give more answers.

What's happening?
What's going on?
What's the problem?
What's wrong with all of us?
Where is this world going?

But I don't have answers. And it turns out that most of the answers we come up with just don't do the trick. When you try to find out where most of those answers come from, it's actually hard to discover, but I definitely don't see them in the Bible.

Every year we celebrate Lent at Branches. Lent (which precedes Easter on the church calendar) is a time of year when we really stop trying to answer questions and just acknowledge that we don't have them. It's a season where we acknowledge that trees don't have leaves and that we are tired of the cold weather, snow, and lack of life all around us.

Whoever planned for Lent to be at the end of winter was a genius.

Our second year we took out all the chairs, put up big blackboards, and had people write out their frustrations, complaints, doubts, and rants to God. After the service, the text on those boards was overwhelmingly honest and beautiful and sobering and freeing. It was one of the most memorable Sundays we ever had, and there was no sermon or answers or telling everyone that "everything is going to be alright."

About five months ago I started looking at the book of Ecclesiastes for our third season of Lent. I had read it before and heard sermons on it, but I wanted to reread it with all the new questions in mind.

What I found blew me away. It's audacious, revolutionary, and radical stuff. The fact that it is in the Bible is hardly believable. It was big. It was mind shifting and world altering. It was important.

That guy on the bike trail.

That owner in Ellensburg.

Those caribou in Labrador.

And all the other stories.

What's happening?
What's going on?
What's the problem?
What's wrong with all of us?
Where is this world going?

Well, Ecclesiastes has answers, but they aren't the answers that we are used to, and they aren't the answers that we usually give. They aren't the boring, cliché Christian answers, and they aren't cynical or judgmental. They are optimistic, but in an unexpected way. And they aren't always sure of themselves.

They are more raw, liberating, moving, mysterious, inspiring, authentic, beautiful, and creative.

In fact, the answers aren't really even answers, which is maybe the best part about them because there are certain people—and certain ways of living—that just don't seem to *need* the answers.

They're just too busy living and breathing everything in around them to have time for silly arguments about answers.

two

yacine.

From the second he walks in to Starbucks, he's different. He walks with a confidence and stature that most want, but don't have, so they fake it. But you can smell it miles away when they do. Money, power, and everything that goes with it—well, we want the authentic version.

It's been said that in the same way we all have a physical body, we also have a body of energy. There are certain people that enter a room and physically they might be muscular, tall, short, or skinny, but it doesn't matter because energetically they are huge and everyone is aware of them in *that* sense. Their "presence" is large and it fills the space and hits some kind of other sensors in our body that detect *that* kind of energy. We say things like "she just lights up the room" and "there's something different about him" and "they bring an energy . . ." for a reason.

There are some people who can dance or sing or speak or act.

There are others who can dance or sing or speak or act who have "it".

He has *it*.

Physically, he looks on the older side of middle age. His hair is mostly black with some tinges of white, and his skin color is the same as mine at the end of summer—and after being outside a lot. Actually, his is still better. I'm a little jealous of that kind of skin. He looks Middle Eastern.

But none of that really matters because he has that energy; it envelops me. I'm mesmerized. I don't really care what he looks like.

He introduces himself and tells me his name is Yacine.

Thirty seconds into our conversation, I know I will never meet another person like him. Ever.

Five minutes into our conversation, I'm about to tell him that he needs some serious counseling and that I'm not the person to do it. He comes across as mentally unstable, at best—suicidal, at worst—and, either way, in desperate need of some help. I am not the man for this job.

What's happening?
What's going on?
What's the problem?
What's wrong with all of us?
Where is this world going?

It's all he says over and over in different ways than I've heard before, but it's still depressing. It's all meaningless and worthless. Life. Everything. "What's the point of doing anything, or what's the point of even going on?" he asks.

Real exciting stuff. But he has *that* energy. I keep listening. And then he really starts to grab me with his stories. I quickly become enamored, intoxicated, and addicted.

Yacine is beyond rich. Millions. No, billions. He talks about his private planes—more than one. He has a few smaller jets, but usually he travels on a 767, which is the same jet that holds over 300 people and flies from Los Angeles to London for the airlines. He talks about his private yachts; his largest is over 140 meters. He talks about the staffs that live on his yachts and bring them to any spot on the globe that he wants them to, where he meets them, usually with his 767, if the airport he is going to is large enough to handle his 767. Otherwise, he brings his smaller jet. He tells me about islands east of New Zealand that I didn't know existed. He owns a few islands—entire land masses surrounded by white sand beaches. He owns them and goes there whenever he wants.

He talks about houses in Milan, Hong Kong, Paris, New York, Seattle, Houston, Sydney, Melbourne, Stockholm, and other places. I ask him about Sweden because it's a country I've always wanted to visit, and he tells me he has two houses in Sweden. One in Stockholm and another at a ski resort that I don't remember. His parents had him skiing every year in Europe since the time he could walk.

He doesn't remember ever *not* skiing. He doesn't remember a time when he didn't do most things.

He talks about businesses: oil, technology, investment, and art. He bought a painting in 2010 for $28 million just because he could. After this statement, I wonder why he didn't treat me to coffee.

He talks about women. He has women who are paid to live in the houses year round just so they are there when he arrives. *If* he arrives.

He has twelve wives scattered throughout the world. But he tells me that his wives are more for show and for children than for sex. He talks about sex with other women—exotic, beautiful, international women. I prod—even though I'm a man with one wife whom I love intensely and who is beautiful and exotic. I don't really talk to—much less have sex with—multiple exotic, beautiful, international women. The whole concept is beyond me. I push him on details. He offers me one story, only so we can move on, of five Italian models who begged him to have sex with them. He met them at a party and they pleaded to come home with him (probably the Milan home). So he obliged. "All five at the same time." He says it was "fun" with the same amount of enthusiasm that I used to say playing *Candyland* with my four-year-old was "fun."

I get the impression he has other stories, but he knows that's all someone of my caliber needs to be impressed. We quickly move on.

He talks about education. He has two PhDs—one in mathematics and another in neuroscience. And he has another one, that doesn't really count, in religion. That was just for "fun." I wonder if that's the same kind of fun as being with five women at the same time. I don't even know what I want the answer to be. He has taught at Cambridge, the University of Hong Kong, and the University of Sydney in permanent positions and numerous other places for shorter terms.

He never stays long at any of the places because he gets bored teaching uninteresting topics to uninteresting people. Did I say he had a house in Sydney as well?

He talks about armies. He's a prince of some kind (he's a little vague when it comes to this). He talks about guards and legions and elite US-trained commando units at his disposal. He talks about meeting presidents and prime ministers and dictators and secret deals that you only hear about in movies. I ask him if the United States government really buys luxury cars in exchange for phone numbers like they did in *Zero*

Dark Thirty and he just smiles—like a parent smiles at a kid who asks if it's true that people sometimes hurt each other on purpose.

He talks about religion. He has studied them all and taught each of them. He is a man of faith, a man of God, a man of morality and spirituality and goodness. He understands Buddhism, Islam, Judaism, Hinduism and Christianity. He quotes for me passages from the Koran, the Torah, the Bhagavad Gita, and the Bible.

He tells me that he doesn't care if anyone has heard of him or not. He doesn't need to care because when you're as rich and powerful as he is, you don't need anyone to affirm you. You've already been affirmed in every way that a society can offer affirmation.

He tells me that it's those who are still trying to climb the mountain who need you to know they have almost made it to the top. But when you get to the top, the view changes.

Then he starts telling me about boukhar. "Everything is boukhar," he says, over and over, in Starbucks. He yells it so loud that it's on the verge of being embarrassing.

And then we're no longer on the verge; we're well *into* embarrassing. I start looking around and I smile at the people who are staring at us. I wonder, again, if he does need serious psychological help. Yacine is all about boukhar—the Arabic word for vapor. But Yacine says it's more than that. It's fog. It's smoke. It's breath. It's an old word with many meanings, and all of those meanings are needed to understand the word. It's something you can't grab a hold of. It's something that always manages to escape your grasp.

And then he really starts to get into it (as if he wasn't earlier).

He says that everything is boukhar, and everything has no point. He asks me why we work and what I gain from working. He asks me what the point of working is. I would like to tell him that it's money, but he would just laugh at me.

He tells me people are born and people die, that generations come and generations go, and only the land and the sky and the mountains and the seas remain.

He tells me to look at the sun. I try, but we're inside. He says to think about how it rises and sets, and to look at the wind and where it blows. "What is the point," he asks again?

I don't really have an answer. I never do.

He starts talking about rivers and how they flow into the ocean, yet the ocean never fills up. Do you ever feel like a river? I realize I have never asked myself that question. He talks about weather using concepts from elementary school. He talks about evaporation—about water going back into the clouds and then coming back again onto the ground and into the rivers and into the ocean that never fills up. I see those little, curved arrows pointing to clouds and oceans that are on white boards and in textbooks.

He talks about cycles.

He says everything is exhausting, and we're all tired. From what? Why are we so tired? We never see enough; we never hear enough; we're all trying to do something new and there is nothing new left to do. We can't come up with anything new or unique or awe-inspiring. We wear ourselves out seeking something that can't be found. It's all been done before.

I ask him about the iPhone 5 and he laughs at me.

"Yes, we can suddenly talk and schedule and entertain ourselves. We could never do that before," he answers, very sarcastically.

I'm about to tell him how much *easier* it is now. Does he know I paid for our coffee with my iPhone by simply holding it in a certain way? I decide to keep my mouth shut.

He says to think about the Starbucks we are in and try to imagine it a thousand years ago. Who was there? What were they doing? What were they tiring themselves out for?

I imagine some Native Americans who spoke Salish and who probably called a certain area "Children of the Sun." I imagine them fishing, laughing, smoking, having sex, taking care of their babies, planting crops, looking at sunsets. I then realize all of that would have been just a few hundred years ago. I have no idea who or what was in our spot a *thousand* years ago.

But Yacine says to think of all of the things that consumed whatever humans there were here or near here. Think about their worries and their fears or their desires and their joys. Think about how they worried about their children or their grand-children and the legacy they would leave.

They have left no legacy. They have given us nothing. They are boukhar. Gone, like the wind that blew through here yesterday. They have left into the dirt, only to return to the air and be forgotten just like the rain. It goes into the river and never fills up.

Cycles.

We do not even speak their same language. If they came here today we would not even be able to communicate with them.

Then he asks me to think of us sitting in that Starbucks and to ask ourselves what we are consumed with. "Think of this spot 1,000 years from now.

"No one will know that we talked here, that we sat here, that we discussed the meaning of the world. No one will know our children or our grand-children or our great, great, great-grandchildren." He talks about books I want to write and laughs again. "So what? You will write books that no one will be able to read in the language you wrote them 1,000 years from now. And do you really think what you write will have any meaning 1,000 years from now?

"There will be other great pastors, other great speakers, other great writers, other great fathers, other great husbands, other great men of faith—or men of science—and other great game designers who turn into pastors because they think they saw burning bushes.

"What is the point of all of these things that we see?"

At this point, I take a sip of green tea, but I imagine that if I had a gun I would just go ahead and shoot myself right then and there to end all of the boukhar once and for all.

He's depressing, and he keeps going. And I keep listening. Energy.

He tells me about studying in the great universities of the world. He talks about traveling the world and seeing everything that is being done in science, faith, medicine, and technology. He says that "Humanity is weighed down by the pressure of imaginary gods to do something great," and that he has seen everything done, everywhere.

He says he has become wise. He has read books, heard speeches from Nobel Prize winners, and taught classes to the brightest minds and intellects on our planet. They have been stunned at what he knows and that *they* do not know.

He has taken years to focus on wisdom. On knowledge. On more education. He has taken years to focus on fools. To learn what makes them fail and fall.

"All of it is boukhar," he keeps saying, over and over. Vapor. Breath.

Then he starts talking about pleasure, which really perks me up again. He says it has taken him years to find the greatest pleasures on Earth. He spent ten years pursuing pleasure, wherever it took him.

Pleasure, wherever it took him. That sounds . . . good?

He talks about wine, women, cars, planes, travel, buildings, businesses, success . . . and the fact that there was not one thing that he denied himself. Not *one* thing.

I actually ask "Not *one* thing?" and he replies "Not *one* thing."

We both know what that means.

Who am I kidding? I have no idea what that means.

He tells me that the best wine I've ever tasted is water compared to what he has had. He laughs again. He says the best sex I can imagine he's had a thousand times. He says the most luxurious, romantic, relaxing, or adventurous vacation I can imagine, he has *lived* for years. He says he has tasted everything that the world has to offer. He says he took his time to embrace what the religions call "the ways of the world."

He embraced foolishness and immorality so that there could be nothing to stop him from overdosing on pleasure—from taking in more pleasure than humans are meant to consume.

And it's all boukhar.

So, he says he tried other things. He wanted to see what people found meaning in.

He built hotels, resorts, and companies. He planted vineyards and won awards for producing the best reds and whites on the planet. (Another dream of mine crushed—no pun intended.) He created gardens and parks for his people. He created groves of fruit tress where fruit trees never grew. He had servants of every kind, and paid them handsomely. He grew golf courses in deserts by watering them twenty-four hours a day. He is paid over $100,000 just for the sperm of horses that he owns. *Kentucky Derby*, *Preakness*, *Melbourne Cup*, and the *Dubai World Cup*: been there, done that.

He starts talking like he is Muhammad Ali. He says that he's the greatest, that he owns the greatest, and that he's held nothing back.

And it is all boukhar.

He says he hated his life. He hated work. He hated all that he had done. He hated chasing these winds and watching the sun rise and fall. He hated all that he had amassed for one simple reason: Who is to say what will happen to it all when he dies? Who will come after him? What will they do?

He talks about how much he has worked, how much effort he has put in—all of the stress and anxiety and toil—and for what? A fool can come along, who has done nothing to earn any of it, and spoil it all.

I almost feel sorry for him at this point. I'm almost thankful that I don't have private jets and houses all over the world.

Almost.

Work, itself, is boukhar. "Why do I work," he says. "Why do I gain? Why do I build and collect and buy?"

"Why, Ryan?"

I don't have an answer. Again.

He talks about grief and pain. He says he can't sleep at night when thinking about what he has and how he can get more. He says he can't be satisfied, even with everything he has done and owns. As he gains more, the monster becomes larger. The monster that can only be fed with his own ambition and desire. It is never full. Never satisfied. It is always hungry.

He says that he looks at those who work for him, who are paid nothing (especially compared to him) and yet they sleep with peace. They eat little, but they rest. He pauses for a while on this thought.

"They rest," he repeats.

I think of the caribou: "Born into a life of perpetual motion, this newborn had to run within hours to keep pace."

"All I have, all I own, all I have done, it does not even allow me to rest, Yacine says.

At this point, it's no longer Yacine who needs counseling; I wonder if I do. I once heard Macklemore say that he might have been happier before *Thrift Shop* went big than after.[3] I didn't know fame and success got *this* bad. We all know money doesn't buy happiness, but I didn't think it bought suicide.

Yacine keeps talking for a little longer. He's now talking about "one more thing," which reminds me of Steve Jobs who used to always end his announcements with the same line. I wonder, for a moment, if Steve Jobs would have said the same things as Yacine.

Yacine says that "The faithful and the wise and the spiritual and the religious and those who consider wisdom to be the thing that you can hold onto as the thing that matters . . ." He laughs. "To the answers", he says, and raises his cup of coffee as though it were the world's finest Merlot.

"It, too, is nothing, and has no point. The answers have no point. The points have no point."

He has studied the fools. He has studied the mad. He has studied the immoral and the lazy and the hedonistic. He has studied the wise and the religious and the spiritual. He has seen the fool walk into the cave and never return, and he has seen the wise bring a light with them.

"But, in the end, what is the point? Both of them will die." Yacine says that he "will die like a fool; he will die like a mad man; he will die as the immoral and the lazy and the hedonistic die. We all die the same way. Fate waits for us all, and not one of us will be remembered in 1,000 years."

It is all boukhar.

He finally stops. He's breathing heavily, almost exhausted and tired, which makes sense to me. I've only been listening and I am tired.

What *was* the point?

I probe for a little more information on the boukhar and ask: "What do you mean?"

"I have already told you. The word is Arabic. It means vapor. Smoke. Breath. Imagine this room filling with clouds and vapors and breath."

I do. I imagine a smoke machine filling up Starbucks like a night club. I imagine *Big Pimpin'* playing on the stereo system. I think of the older lady in the corner with her tall Caramel Macchiato and the look of horror that would be on her face if Starbucks literally turned into a night club. I smile, but Yacine brings me back. He says to "imagine the vapors all around." They are so visible and tangible and right there, yet when I try to grab them I can't ever hold them. I imagine myself going insane just trying to grab anything, just one handful of smoke, and I think of those caribou again.

He tells me to imagine the vapors filling the room even more. They consume me and Yacine and all of us who are in the store. They are all we see, but we still can't *hold* them. We lose sight of everyone else. We miss them because of the vapors that consume our thoughts and vision.

I am blind because of something that I can't even touch.

I think of that owner in Ellensburg again. Blind to his employees and their views of him as he dies with all of his money.

Yacine smiles and tells me "There are many people in this world. Some of them are young and they look at the vapors from afar, imagining what their life will be like when they get them.

"Some are in the middle of the clouds of smoke, only discovering now that all of their dreams were nothing but imaginations. They are trying to grab them, to feel them, to feel anything, but there is never anything there. They are numb from the effects.

"Some are old. They have found it all to be meaningless. Pointless. Vapors. They are at the end and wondering what it was all for."

It all reminds me of reading André Agassi's biography *Open*. He said that he was in *vapor lock*. Boukhar lock. Consuming yet empty. Always calling but never letting us catch it. I imagined what it looks like in my own life, to be locked on the meaningless, pointless boukhar.

But then Yacine catches me off guard. He says that boukhar is not evil. He tells me to close my eyes and feel the heat from my nostrils. He tells me to "imagine this air coming into my nose, into my lungs, and converting into oxygen that feeds my body through my blood, reaching to every cell from the top of my scalp to the end of my toes.

"In and out. The breath that gives you everything, and yet you never stop to even acknowledge that it is there. Everything breathes!" he yells.

"Everything breathes," he repeats.

"Breath is life. But if you chase the breath, it is meaningless boukhar. You can be dead even as you breathe life. Dead with life surrounding you."

He ends with this idea of wisdom. There is "old wisdom" that talks about two paths, two choices, methods, formulas, concepts, diagrams, and self-help books. But he has wisdom for another level. Something deeper. Something more real. Not the answers that end up being boukhar. He says he has found true wisdom and asks me to listen. He will teach and I will be the student.

I'm ready.

Alright, so none of that happened, which is probably pretty obvious. I do, however, have a friend named Yacine, and he is an Arab. Other than that, the meeting with Yacine was fictional. And yet, it's not altogether fiction. The book Ecclesiastes was written thousands of years ago by a guy who, if he showed up today at a Starbucks, would be a lot like—and sound a lot like—Yacine. In fact, everything Yacine said is simply my version of sections taken directly from Ecclesiastes.

Just reading Solomon's book, at first glance, is maddening. It's common to think the guy should have been in the psychiatric ward. But then, it starts to hit home. Solomon and the words of the Teacher (which is what Solomon calls himself) start to sink in and penetrate and affect everything.

The American novelist Thomas Wolfe once called Ecclesiastes "the noblest, the wisest, and the most powerful expression of man's life upon this earth—and also the highest flower of poetry, eloquence, and truth," as well as "the greatest single piece of writing I have ever known, and the wisdom expressed in it the most lasting and profound."[4]

I'm not sure the praise gets any bigger than that and I agree completely.

As amazing as the book is, the story of the author is just as amazing and important. I don't think it's possible to make a modern day character as wealthy, as powerful, and as famous as Solomon was, without us laughing at it. We wouldn't believe it. But in the third century BC this man, Solomon, was *the* man.

He had it all. Yacine-times-ten.

He had armies, palaces, horses, goats, slaves, wives (around 700), concubines (around 300), and the Queen of Sheba coming to visit. From what I understand, if you had the Queen of Sheba coming to visit, you were a lucky man.

But maybe the greatest thing about Solomon is the story of him and his dream. In the dream, God comes to Solomon and tells him he can have anything in the world. Anything. Solomon says he wants a discerning heart to govern and to distinguish between right and wrong. God is so impressed that Solomon doesn't ask for death for all his enemies or land rights in Egypt, that God says he will make Solomon the wisest person to ever live—meaning no one has ever been as wise and no one will ever be—and give him all the other stuff, too.

Then Solomon wakes up from his dream. Maybe.[5]

Guy in the cycling jersey.
Owner in Ellensburg.
Caribou in Canada.

What's happening?
What's going on?
What's the problem?
What's wrong with all of us?
Where is this world going?

Well, we have a guy with more money, more women, more power, and more achievements than, arguably, any human being who has ever lived, and who supposedly gets more wisdom from God than anyone who will ever live. And this guy writes a book which gives us answers that don't match most of the answers that many of the people who follow the same God would give.

Yeah it's *that* good. How can you not love *that*?

three

islands.

It's a wicked, toxic, hellish island. Black rock erupts from a putrid, swirling ocean while ominous storm clouds roll in the air above. Waves crash against its jagged shore and lightning tears into its rough, mountainous terrain. The tips of sharp trees scattered against its silhouette make it look like a mouth ready to tear into anyone who approaches.

It's a dark, cold, ominous, and, generally, *very* unwelcoming place.

It is on this island where everything from irritating to bad to sad to tragic to horrific occurs.

It is on this island where . . .

He enters an elementary school and murders innocent children.

She discovers she has stage four cancer at the age of twenty-seven.

He decides to take a nap in the afternoon and never wakes up, leaving his wife and children with no chance to say goodbye.

The debt piles up, the car accident happens, and he is still single even though he wants nothing more in life than to find a partner.

He still can't forgive himself for what he did to those innocent people in the Vietnamese village.

The loneliness gets so heavy and thick that it's hard to function. A bottle of pills are a better option than his wife and son.

She dates him for two years and believes "he's the one" only to find out he has found another "her."

She can't get pregnant no matter what they try and how much money they throw at it.

The divorce comes after twenty-three years of marriage, and it comes via a text message.

They pick up the shattered hearts and emotions of the kids and try to put them back together, knowing it will never happen.

While it's hard—maybe impossible—to gauge tragedies or pain or sadness, especially for those who find themselves in the middle of them, not all darkness on this island is at the far end of the spectrum.

It is also there where the dishwasher breaks, the flu wreaks havoc, the unexpected bill arrives, the pay cut hurts, and the homework is overwhelming.

It all happens on that island.

But there is another island. Red rock, covered with lush green vegetation, erupts from a turquoise ocean with light dashes of white clouds floating harmlessly in a bright blue sky. Soft tides lick the white sands, and bulbous, sweet fruits grow like weeds.

It's a colorful, warm, propitious, and, generally, very welcoming place.

It is on this island where everything from nice to good to happy to fantastic to perfect (or as close as it gets) occurs.

It is on this island where . . .

She is offered the job of her dreams right out of college because the employer happened to see that paper she wrote.

She finds him in Europe, and their first kiss is as the sun is setting on top of the Eiffel Tower.

He wins the lottery with the first ticket he bought at the gas station where he works.

She holds the college degree and smiles for the photo with her wonderful, supportive parents.

A few bottles of wine and best friends sit on a deck on a hot summer night.

They find the house in the classified section of the newspaper and cry with delight when they walk in the front door because "it's just what we wanted."

The doctor looks up from the ultrasound with a huge smile and says "twins!"

He marries her before going to Normandy and they still walk hand-in-hand in Central Park after seventy-five years of bliss.

The painting, book, or song . . . it just comes together. It's a magic moment of creativity direct from the gods.

Peace, contentment, joy, satisfaction, pleasure, wisdom, and happiness thrive.

While it's hard—maybe impossible—to gauge gifts or healing or happiness, especially for those who find themselves in the middle of them, not all beauty on this island is at the far end of the spectrum.

It is also there where the flights are smooth, the weather is just what everyone hoped it would be, the game is won, the kiss is magic, the food is delightful, and she says "I love you, Daddy" before bed.

It all happens on that island.

Between these islands is a wide ocean and on that ocean is a boat. It's a small boat, like those little row boats that most kids used to jump in with friends at summer camp. It's got two oars and it's just wide enough where one person can't grab both oars at the same time. It's also got a little sail. It goes up and down pretty easily with a convenient pulley system. Nothing fancy, but very functional.

Imagine yourself on that boat. That ominous, vicious island can be seen far in the distance, and that beautiful, tropical paradise is just as far away. In fact, the boat is floating directly between the two spots. Everything within us, and around us, tells us to do everything we can to be as *far* away from that dark island and as *close* to that beautiful island as we can get. Hopefully, if we're lucky, they say we'll eventually land the boat on those white sands.

So we row.

But there are other forces at play. There are currents that sometimes take us toward the dark and sometimes toward the light. There is wind that sometimes takes us in the opposite direction. And we have many names for these forces: God, destiny, fate, morality, the world, society, culture, or choice. Depending on your point of view, these forces are trying to take us toward light island or toward dark island—or both, or either, or neither.

It is here, on that ocean, that we start to find all kinds of formulas and world views.

There are those who say if you row hard enough, you will get to light island. What they often mean is that the current is laziness or weakness and if you just row strong enough and long enough, you can fight what-ever it is and get to light island. You'll win, and if you don't win . . . well . . . you didn't deserve to win. You didn't earn it.

There are those who say that if you get that sail in just the right spot and catch the wind, it will take you to light island. What they often mean is that the wind is God, and if you put that sail up, you can catch God who is always trying to get you to light island because that's what God is about. Which means if you find yourself moving toward dark island . . . well . . . God isn't with you.

But there are other views. There are those who say that the current is the morality of the world and you have to make better choices to row against "the world" and find the wind of God.

And sometimes people say that God takes us to dark island in order to teach us a lesson.

And sometimes people say that the current is the world or society or culture or science, and that the world is taking us to light island. If we just listen to society and what we've learned, and ignore religion, we'll find ourselves where we want to be.

And sometimes people say that you have to be careful because life isn't about being happy or getting to any island.

This gets very confusing, very fast. Where is God, what is good, what is bad, what forces are pushing us where we *don't* want to go, and what forces are pulling us where we *do* want to go? Sometimes none of them are and sometimes all of them are, and we find ourselves in the middle of the ocean working . . . very . . . hard.

Very hard.

We're exhausted because it *is* exhausting. We're drained, spent, tired, trying to figure out how to leverage whatever it is we're supposed to leverage and whatever it is we're supposed to fight and whatever it is we're supposed to believe or pray or read or buy or ignore or watch.

Most of the time it seems as though everyone is telling us something different.

Atheists. Christians. Sociologists. Advertisers. Facebook posts. Bloggers. Journalists. Movies. Television. Buddhists. Singers. Celebrities. Muslims. Psychologists. Counselors. Pastors. Teachers. Friends. Enemies. Politicians.

And we haven't even talked about the boat. The boat is the key, others will say. It's the boat that gets us *there*.

It's the boat that will bring us to the light and away from the dark.

Yahoo!

It's the boat that will bring us to the dark and away from the light.

Oh no!

This boat gets called all kinds of things as well. God. Wealth. Fame. Power. Religion. Knowledge. Wisdom. Education. Faith. Works. Generosity. Morality. Rule. Law. Government. Church.

And *this* just makes this whole concept all the *more* complicated.

Maybe God is the boat. But what is the wind? Maybe God is the wind and wealth is the boat. Does God want us to be wealthy? Some say yes, some say no, some say there is no God so who cares?

Maybe power is the boat. Or the currents? Maybe government is the boat that will take us *there*? Or are the elected leaders the ones ru-ining everything? Corruption and greed. We need less government! More government! No government! We need God in government. We need God out of government. We need to start working more. Working less. Working better. More faith. Less faith. No faith. More education. We need to change education. Better systems. We need revolution! We need compliance.

And *then* we'll get *there*.

But I'm so tired of trying.

We are left with more rowing, more working to get the sail just right, more sweating whenever we near dark island, and more smiles whenev-er we near light island. But no matter where we are, we are desperate to do something to get us away or closer.

Of course, we start to look at others who have "arrived" at one of the islands and we start to think things about them . . . and us . . .

They made it. Will I?

They didn't. What does that mean?

They earned it. Can I?

They lost it. I can't let that happen.

They have God on their side. Which God?

They have the devil on their side. Do they think it's God?

They are a success. I want to be one, too.

They are a failure. They didn't want it bad enough. It was their destiny. God is teaching them a lesson.

They didn't do enough, believe enough, think enough, have enough faith . . . in the *right* things.

They did too much, believed too much, thought about too much, had too much faith . . . in the *wrong* things.

We judge them and we judge ourselves based not on how any of us actually lives, but on the apparent results of the formulas.

Everyone keeps offering more voices to this whole story and many of them are just more formulas that often seem to be somehow related to those boats, the islands, currents, and winds.

And . . .

If light island is where life resides and dark island is where destruction resides, then we have to figure this out.

Right now.

Everything depends on it.

The stress and effort of figuring this out are palpable. Talk to people and feel it. Walk around an airport and see it. Take a drive and taste it.

We are those caribou, but we don't even know where we're migrating to. It feels like we're running around in circles and coming back to the grasses that we were just at, that we've already eaten, and we're starving. For something. Yet, no one seems to be figuring anything out. No one seems to have this nailed down in any way and that includes:

Atheists. Christians. Sociologists. Advertisers. Facebook posts. Bloggers. Journalists. Movies. Television. Buddhists. Singers. Celebrities. Muslims. Psychologists. Counselors. Pastors. Teachers. Friends. Enemies. Politicians.

But what if there is no boat? Really, at the end of the day, when you boil it down, that boat is some kind of a formula. The boat is some *way* to get some *place* by doing some *thing*. If that boat is some kind of formula then it contains the two words that all formulas are built on: if, then.

If I . . .

get enough money,

have enough faith,

do enough good things,

reject God,

accept God,

stop sinning,

get that job,

get that house,

find that wife,

find that husband,

discover the secret to life and wisdom and knowledge,

finish that book,

see that country,

kiss that girl,

have that child,

win that championship,

read the Bible,

pray,

give up religion,

discover science,

then I will . . .

>be happy, content, at peace, successful, elated, joyful, healthy, and living.

Whatever our "if, then" is, it's the boat. And whatever our boat is, it's an idol. It's not only religious people who have idols. We all do. An idol is just that *thing* that we think will take us away from sad and toward happy if we worship or serve the thing in just the right way.

Formulas are idols. Idols are formulas.

The ironic thing is that many religious people have views of a God that will take them away from sad and toward happy if they treat that God right, which means that their view of God is not actually God at all, but just another idol. This means that some of the people that like to spend a lot of time pointing out "idols" like sex, drugs, and rock 'n roll might actually have a much bigger problem with idols themselves—a view of God that is the wrong view.

This is probably why Jesus said things along the lines of "before you start pointing out the problems with other people and how they see the world, you might want to look at how you see the world yourself, especially if you're claiming to follow God."[6]

Surrounding the story of the Ten Commandments is an interesting story. Moses is up on a mountain while God is etching words onto some rocks. But while Moses is up on the mountain, all of the people who are following Moses start getting tired of "waiting for God" and so they collect everyone's jewelry and make a golden cow.

The crazy thing is that the golden cow is supposed to represent the God they are tired of waiting for up on the mountain, who is handing out guidelines for living; the first, of which, says don't have any idols.[7] They make an idol not because they want a *new* God, but because they want the God they believe in to be more present and do the things they want a God to do.

They want a vending machine.

They want a formula so they create an idol. In other words, what we see today from people who claim to follow this same God is not a new thing.

But, of course, it's not just religious people; it's all of us. We all have *that* thing that will make us feel *that* way if we can *just* get enough of *it*.

And it never works. Those boats are just representations of ideas that don't exist in reality.

What if the islands don't exist either?

What if there is no happy place, just as there is no sad place?

What are you working for? What are you afraid of?

What if it's so confusing and so exhausting and so cyclical because none of it is real? What if the only place any of these happy and sad places exist is in our heads? What if there is no wind and there are no currents? What if all of this exhaustion is from fighting forces and battles that don't even exist either?

> *When times are good, be happy; but when times are bad, consider this: God has made the one as well as the other. Therefore, no one can discover anything about their future.*[8]

> *Light is sweet, and it pleases the eyes to see the sun. However many years anyone may live, let them enjoy them all. But let them remember the days of darkness, for there will be many. Everything to come is meaningless.*[9]

(By the way, whenever Solomon uses the word "meaningless," it's more like boukhar—vapors. It's the Hebrew word *hevel*, and it's also translated as empty, vain, futile, breath, and vapor.)

Solomon seemed to see the world (reality) differently. As Solomon looked out over the world, he seemed alright with the fact that there is light and dark and it's here. Good, happy, bad, light, sweet, and darkness. It's all right here, right now. There is no getting *there* or staying *away* from somewhere else.

It's all *here* whether we like it or not. There aren't two islands; there is one, and it's called reality—and we all live there.

What would all of this mean?

Just imagine it for a second.

What if that were true?

What if

> all that rowing,
> all that pushing,
> all that fighting,
> all that coercing,
> all the effort,
> for currents
> and sails
> and wind

will *never* succeed?

What if the reason we're so exhausted is because we're working so hard to get *away* from a place and *to* another place that we will never find anywhere?

And we hear glimpses of this all the time. Studies tell us that money doesn't make us as happy as we think. Of course, when money can buy basic needs to survive (food, shelter, water), rich countries are happier than poor countries, but beyond that "Once a society's level of per capita wealth crosses a threshold from poverty to adequate subsistence, further increases in national wealth have almost no affect on happiness."[10]

No affect?

We hear glimpses of it in stories like Andre Agassi's. He was the number one-ranked tennis player in the world who owned his own jet and was about to get married to a supermodel who graduated from Princeton. This guy had things going so well that when he wore a pair of Oakley sunglasses during a tennis match because of a hangover, the president of Oakley sent him a truck load of sunglasses to say thanks.[11]

You could say that for whatever reason, his boat was sailing to the right island. Sometimes, literally. "I gaze at the palm trees, the foaming coastline, the misty rain forests, and think: another island paradise. Why do we always feel compelled to run off to island paradises? It's as though we have Blue Lagoon Syndrome."[12]

But then he says, "I fantasize about the engine sputtering, the plane spiraling down into the mouth of a volcano. To my chagrin, we land safely.[13]

What's that? Come again? You don't like island paradises so much that you wish you would die? Agassi later says, "I hate tennis more than ever—but I hate myself more."[14]

How can you hate yourself when you have so much going for you?

We hear glimpses of it in the pastor and the celebrity and the counselor. We hear that the fame, or power, or cars, or women, or stuff don't bring us happiness.

But maybe none of those actually take it far enough? What if those solutions are just scratching the surface?

Maybe the problem isn't money or our quest for it, but it's that we still think there are these places that exist, and if we just do something— anything—we can get to one of them and stay away from the other.

And that's just not true.

Not with money. Or religion.

Anthony de Mello was a Jesuit priest who lived in India and is probably one of my favorite thinkers, philosophers, and writers to ever live. He writes the following:

> "What, concretely, is Enlightenment?"

"'Seeing Reality as it is,' said the Master."

"Doesn't everyone see Reality as it is?"

"Oh, no! Most people see it as they think it is."

"What's the difference?"

"The difference between thinking you are drowning in a stormy sea and knowing you cannot drown because there isn't any water in sight for miles around."[15]

If enlightenment is simply acknowledging what life *really* is and not what we *think* it is, we should definitely figure out what life really is. To that end, and keeping this whole island analogy going, Solomon says we should start by acknowledging there is one island and we live on it.

Which means . . .

There is no getting there.

There is no staying away from there.

There is no finding the right current or belief, or catching the right wind or faith, or getting the right boat or formula that will ensure we're always on the winning team and never on the losing one.

And if that's true, this means that . . .

exhaustion

and struggle

and fighting . . .

well . . .

I don't have to do it anymore.

Ahhh. I'm not drowning. In fact, there's no water in sight.

Maybe there are some more truths to the way life works on this island. Maybe there are some practical things to do to survive on it. Maybe there is a lot more encouragement and relief and freedom to be found right here, where we all live together, once we start acknowledging the reality of it all.

four

pain.

A plane takes off from Orlando, Florida, with a flight plan to Virginia. At 13,000 feet, the plane starts to leak oil which eventually splatters all over the windshield, making it difficult for the pilot to see. Eventually, the propeller comes off, and the pilot is forced to make an emergency landing on a beach.

Robert Gary Jones was a pharmaceutical sales representative on a business trip in North Carolina. He was on the last day of the trip, about ready to fly home and celebrate his daughter's third birthday. He also had a five-year-old son.

Robert Gary Jones decided to go for a jog on the beach near where he was staying. He plugged in his iPod, put on some music, and started running shortly after six in the evening.

The pilot of the plane forced to make an emergency landing did not see Robert; and Robert did not hear the plane since the plane was flying without a propeller and Robert was listening to music. The plane hit Robert, killing him instantly.

Some people called the landing "miraculous."

The mother of Robert Gary Jones said "They say that God only gives you what you can handle. You know what . . . I've reached my max."[16]

Miraculous? All I can handle?

A piece of rock about 55 feet in diameter and weighing in at 10,000 tons was flying through space at about 40,000 miles per hour. Scientists say the rock originated in an asteroid belt between Mars and Jupiter and had spent 4.5 billion years in space. That rock came to our planet on February 18, 2013. Scientists say that it hit with the force of 300 to 500 kilotons. For most of us, that doesn't mean much; however, the bomb the United States dropped on Hiroshima hit with 16 kilotons.[17]

So this rock hit with at least 20 times the force of an atomic bomb that killed, according to most historians, at least 90,000 people in 1945. This rock sent out a shockwave that circled the globe *twice*.[18]

The piece of rock traveling through space for 4.5 billion years came out of nowhere. No one predicted its arrival. From entry to disintegration was 32.5 seconds. Scientists say we can expect this kind of thing every 100 years. The "blast" injured 1,200 people, two of which were critically injured.

But no one died.

The Prime Minister of Russia said, "Thank God no one died."[19]

Thank God?

It was 4:20 in the morning in Las Vegas. A man was driving a black Range Rover and ended up in an altercation of some kind, which led to shots being fired. The man in the Range Rover shot at another man driving a red Maserati, killing the driver of the Maserati instantly. The Maserati, now without a driver, continued moving and sped through an intersection and into a taxi cab.

A woman was getting into that taxi. She was a two-time breast cancer survivor with three kids. She was in Las Vegas for a trade show because she owned a small boutique in the Pacific Northwest. She left behind a husband and three children when the Maserati killed her and the taxi driver—a 62-year-old man.[20]

I found out about the story at church one morning. During some songs, I noticed a student was crying. I asked her if she was alright, and she said she wasn't. She told me some of the story and said that the woman who had been killed had been like a mom to her.

She said she didn't know what to think. She said she didn't blame God. She said she was numb.

She doesn't blame God?

Last week, I listened to a friend who lost his wife about two years ago. I watched him cry and listened to him tell me how hard it *still* was. I listened to him tell me how hard it *still* was on his kids. He told me about family dynamics, insurance dynamics, and this big strong man cried, over and over, right in front of me.

I didn't even know what to say.

As he continued to share his story, another family approached us: a husband, wife, and three kids. The wife had just found out that after receiving chemotherapy, new spots had appeared. It was stage 4.

She's scared. Terrified. Will this woman's husband's story turn out like my friend's story?

I have no answers.

And, of course, these are just a small sample of the stories we all hear, every day. We hear them on the news, we read them on the Internet, we hear them from friends, and some of us experience their darkness firsthand.

Whether we like it or not, the pain is real. I have personally seen it in the trembling lips of friends, tasted it in my own tears, and seen it crush the souls of people I care about. I assume you have as well.

And it seems like whenever the reality of this pain appears, it's often followed by a statement that involves God in some way or another. This pain forces us to ask real and deep questions about life, about human-ity, and about the existence and personality of God—if God does exist.

Does God *make* these events happen?
Does God *allow* these events to happen?
Does God *know* these things are going to happen?
Is it some kind of *devil* that makes them happen?
Is *humanity* to blame?

These, of course, are not new questions. In fact they are probably the oldest questions. Since they have been around a while, we have come up with lots of answers—some more sincere than others.

God's ways are not our ways.

God is dead.

God works all things for good.

God is worthless.

God sees the bigger story.

God miraculously lets a plane land.

God only gives us what we can handle.

God saved us from the meteor.

God isn't to blame.

Those, of course, are just the tip of the iceberg because so many of us are so desperate for the answers.

My wife met a woman at a party. Within minutes of meeting her, my wife learned that a dog had recently attacked her mother and taken a chunk out of the woman's calf muscle. My wife asked if her mother was alright, to which she replied, "Of course! She's a Christian. It was God's plan for that dog to bite her so that she could talk to her friends about God."

God *planned* the dog to bite her? Are Christians *always* okay? Are dog bites now a requirement to talk about God with friends?

Really?

Like the rest of humanity, Christianity has come up with its own set of answers to these questions throughout its history. And while I'm hardly an expert in all of these answers, it seems like there are three main ingredients used in the recipes of most Christian answers.

Blue Print

These answers center around the idea that God controls everything that will happen. It's almost as though it is all laid out on a giant map in God's workshop. Nothing happens that God doesn't want to happen and nothing doesn't happen that God doesn't want to happen. It's all "part of the plan".[21]

This idea can get pretty extreme. Some take this so far as to say that God doesn't even offer forgiveness to all humans because God knows that not all humans will accept that forgiveness. In other words, God's plan is for some people to never accept God. This is called "limited atonement" and it is at a pretty far end of the spectrum but, then again, if God is controlling everything, it makes sense.

In other words, people say that taxi was supposed to be there, at that time, and the breast cancer survivor was supposed to be getting into it because that's how God planned it from before we even knew what taxis were. And if that taxi driver did not "accept God" before he died, well God knew he never would and never offered him forgiveness in the first place.

Free Will

These answers center around the idea that humans have the capacity to choose and, thus, decide their own fate. God has given us the ability to freely decide and, thus, we have the ability to freely decide to bring pain in an infinite number of ways. There are those that would go so far as to say that God does not even *know* the future because the future is open. God may know possibilities but not the actual choices that humans will make.[22] This would be at the opposite end of the spectrum from "limited atonement".

In other words, that plane started leaking oil at 13,000 feet because a human—somewhere, at some point—did something that eventually led to that happening. And God might not have known it was even going to happen.

Mystery

These answers center around the idea that, at the end of the day, we don't know. This is all a mystery. We don't know, can't know, and never will know and shouldn't argue or discuss blue print or free will or anything else. People will often associate this answer with quotes from the book of Job, primarily the end of the story where God says to Job:

"Brace yourself like a man . . ." and then proceeds to ask him a series of questions about running the universe.

In other words, don't even ask why God doesn't save her from cancer. It's not your place and we'll never know anyway.

As main ingredients, these, of course, lead to thousands of recipes taking bits and pieces of each in some form or combination, enough to fill book upon book about the world, God, and pain.

There are still problems. If free will is kryptonite to God (as some would say) what is nature? Can God do anything about that? In the case of the meteor, what if it *had* hit the earth? What about the meteors that do? What about tsunamis, hurricanes, earthquakes, volcanoes, and sinkholes?

What do we do with all of that?

What about forces of evil? Demons and devils. What about forces of good? Angels. Do they exist apart from free will? Do they have power? Do they have their own free will?

And we could fill books, as many have, with *those* answers.

Regardless of any of these combinations, at some point, things start to boil down to two key words: love and power. We start to say things like if God is all-powerful, why does God let things like this happen? Especially if God is all-loving. Doesn't God care? If so, why doesn't God stop it? Maybe there is no God?

Which leads to even more questions.

Is God all-powerful?

Is God all-loving?

What does it mean to be all-powerful?

What does it mean to be all-loving?

Can something be all-loving and all-powerful at the same time?

Does love require freedom?

Does power allow freedom?

Is it possible for anything to have complete power and freedom?

And these lead to even more questions . . . questions that, I think, might be the most important of them all.

Why are we so obsessed with answering these questions? What is it we *really* want to know?

Do we *really* care why the plane started leaking oil at 13,000 feet?

Do we *really* care why the meteor didn't kill millions of people?

Do we *really* care why the Maserati happened to be heading in the breast cancer survivor's direction?

Do we really care if God planned it? Do we really care if God can stop it? Do we really care if it's our fault?

Of course we care. People died, the pain is real and the pain is dark. There is no denying the tragedy and we care about tragedy.

But why?

Do we really want an answer as to why something already happened or do we want something tangible that we can use so we can prevent it from happening again in the future? To us.

Do we really care for *them* or for *us*?

We don't want any pain.

Isn't *that* one of the most real reasons we *care*? *If* we can just figure out why or who to blame, *then* we can start to figure out a way to stop it. Then we can start to figure out how to create that happy island.

If . . .

God could have stopped it . . .

then . . .

I just need to do more for God next time and I will figure out what that "more" is.

If . . .

God doesn't exist . . .

then . . .

I can stop trying to appease God.

If . . .

it's all a part of the plan . . .

then . . .

I don't have to blame myself for not preventing it.

If . . .

there is no plan . . .

then . . .

I have to work harder.

And on and on it goes . . . circling back and around on itself; the answers tying themselves up in knots in our brains and knots in our stomachs, trying to understand and deduce a formula or a method or a technique to stop the pain next time—at least for myself and for those I love, and, maybe, for others.

And this leads us back to Solomon. Keep in mind that when Solomon wrote Ecclesiastes, he was writing to a people who had it figured out. They *knew* what to do to make God happy and what to do to make God mad, what to do to get God on your side and what to do to get God ticked off, and what to do to be blessed and what to do to be cursed.

God was very much in charge and running the show. If they did the right thing, God would pull the good string, if they did the wrong thing, God would pull the bad one.

In other words, they had all the ifs and thens down to a science. They had entire pages of what sacrifices to make when and where and why in order to get God back on your side.[23]

And then Solomon comes along like a bull in their china shop of formulas.

> So I reflected on all this and concluded that the righteous and the wise and what they do are in God's hands, but no one knows whether love or hate awaits them. All share a common destiny— the righteous and the wicked, the good and the bad, the clean and the unclean, those who offer sacrifices and those who do not. As it is with the good, so with the sinful; as it is with those who take oaths, so with those who are afraid to take them.[24]

Solomon uses all kinds of words to describe the people who are "right" and the people who are "wrong." The religious and the non-religious. The good and the bad. Those who do everything you are supposed to do to avoid pain, and those who don't do anything you are supposed to do to avoid pain.

Then he says this:

> This is the evil in everything that happens under the sun: The same destiny overtakes all.[25]

That was not what was supposed to be said. That is still not what is supposed to be said. You just don't hear that one quoted in church a lot. The same thing happens to the right and the wrong, the religious and the non-religious, and the good and the bad?

What?

> *The hearts of people, moreover, are full of evil and there is mad-ness in their hearts while they live, and afterward they join the dead. Anyone who is among the living has hope—even a live dog is better off than a dead lion! For the living know that they will die, but the dead know nothing; they have no further reward, and even their name is forgotten. Their love, their hate and their jealousy have long since vanished; never again will they have a part in anything that happens under the sun . . .*[26]

A living dog is better than a dead lion? What about heaven? What about hell? What about any kind of afterlife?

> *The race is not to the swift or the battle to the strong, nor does food come to the wise or wealth to the brilliant or favor to the learned; but time and chance happen to them all. Moreover, no one knows when their hour will come: As fish are caught in a cruel net, or birds are taken in a snare, so people are trapped by evil times that fall unexpectedly upon them.*[27]

Time and chance? That's the answer? Time and chance happen to them all?

No matter whether you go to church, no matter whether you offer sac-rifices, no matter whether you are a Christian, an atheist, a Muslim, or a Wiccan . . . time and chance happen to us all.

No matter whether you are gay, single, married, celibate, or a prostitute . . . time and chance happen to us all.

No matter whether you are strong, wise, wealthy, brilliant, or learned . . . just a fish caught in a cruel net or a bird in a snare . . . time and chance happen to us all.

No matter whether we think the wind just happened to catch that sail perfectly or those currents are moving us where we want to go . . . time and chance happen to us all.

Time and chance. *This* is the evil.

A woman gets bit by a dog. This is the evil.
A man dies running on a beach. This is the evil.
A woman dies while getting into a taxi. This is the evil.

This is the evil because this is not good. This is not God. This is not ideal.

But it's the reality, no matter who you are or what you do.

Solomon expands on the whole time thing just to make sure we all understand—and also to provide some good lyrics for *The Byrds* and *Color Me Badd* (two groups probably not mentioned in the same sentence very often).

> *There is a time for everything, and a season for every activity under the heavens:*
>
> *a time to be born and*
> *a time to die,*
> *a time to plant and*
> *a time to uproot,*
> *a time to kill and*
> *a time to heal,*
> *a time to tear down and*
> *a time to build,*
> *a time to weep and*
> *a time to laugh,*
> *a time to mourn and*
> *a time to dance,*
> *a time to scatter stones and*
> *a time to gather them,*
> *a time to embrace and*
> *a time to refrain from embracing,*
> *a time to search and*
> *a time to give up,*
> *a time to keep and*
> *a time to throw away,*
> *a time to tear and*
> *a time to mend,*
> *a time to be silent and*
> *a time to speak,*
> *a time to love and*

a time to hate,
a time for war and
a time for peace.[28]

Time and chance happen to us all.

There is a time that oil leaks at 13,000 feet.

There is a time that a rock travels through space for 4.5 billion years and hurts no one.

There is a time *that* taxi is the *wrong* taxi.

On April 15, 2013, two bombs went off at the Boston Marathon. Along with most of the world, I was glued to the never-ending television footage that followed the tragedy. That footage, shows moments of celebration and thrill to finish a race, followed by moments of cowering, crying, and blood. As I looked at the videos for the third or fourth time on the news, time and chance was never more real.

What if he had run faster? Or slower? What if the parents of that 8-year-old hadn't come to the race? What if his girlfriend didn't run? What if he had decided to do it next year instead? What if the cook had not prepared the chicken properly the night before and then she had spent the night with an upset stomach and run just a little slower because of that? One victim's father said his son "was in the wrong place at the wrong time."[29]

Wrong place, wrong time?

There is something incredibly discomforting about it, especially for those of us who have spent years hearing that life doesn't work that way, and more years trying to figure out how to protect ourselves.

And yet . . .

I recently ran into a friend of mine. Her father left her when she was a little girl. Her single mother survived cancer once, but not the second time, leaving her alone with a sibling. There have been run-ins with the law, drug use, and a lot of trying to get her life back together.

My friend was with her girlfriend at a store. Her girlfriend was sobbing and saying things like "I'm so tired of everything going against me." She told me stories of another friend who was "getting away with every-thing," and she began to cry again—big tears streaming down her face while she talked about how unfair it was that their friend was fooling everyone and getting away with it all while they were trying to get their life together and nothing was working.

I thought of all the answers that I know they've heard.

If you hadn't done drugs.

If your mom and dad hadn't gotten divorced.

If you would start going to church.

If you would get a better job.

If you weren't gay.

Then everything would start to get better.

Instead, I looked them both in the eyes and said, "Hey, sometimes life just happens like that. Some people get away with everything and other people don't. But it's okay. Life isn't fair."

Like I said, I don't have the answers. At that point, I felt like I was saying one of the most cliché things that has ever been said when I'm sup-posed to be a pastor with wise, Godly answers for two people who are going through a lot of pain.

Yet, the relief that flooded her face was palpable. I felt the tension and pressure leave, and I saw a smile appear as she repeated to me, "Life isn't fair. You're right."

And as discomforting as time and chance can be, I think it's also one of the most comforting statements on the planet because it means it's not your fault.

It's

not

your

fault.

It's not your fault your parents divorced. It's not your fault your mom died of cancer. It's not your fault the doctors can't figure out what's going on in your lungs. It's not your fault that life is throwing all of the curveballs at you right now, and you feel like you're suffocating.

For some, this has the potential to change everything.

You have cancer? You're not being punished.

You were raped? God isn't mad at you.

Your father died? It wasn't because you didn't pray enough.

You don't have enough food to eat? This wasn't God's plan for you.

You lost your job? It's not because you fired someone you shouldn't have 10 years ago.

There are a tremendous amount of people who don't ever deal with the pain and the tragedy and the darkness because someone, somewhere, told them that somehow, someway, it's their fault.

They were told that God is teaching them a lesson and that what goes around comes around and that karma is a bitch and that you reap what you sow.

If only you had . . .

or had not . . .

then . . .

And they are defeated before they even begin, which means that it's al-most impossible to make a better move or to become something stronger and healed and restored because it's always been . . . your fault and always will be . . . your fault.

We're humans. Most of us know what works and what doesn't. What we don't know is whether or not, at our core, at the base of who we are, if there is hope and enough strength so that we can start doing more of what works and less of what doesn't.

Time and chance happening can be the best thing to ever hear.

This is fantastic news for the survivors as well. What about the people who don't get cancer, who don't get in the car accident, or who don't lose a child?

I heard an interview with a woman who had run the Boston Marathon, and she said she had been running on the left side of the street (where the bombs went off) but decided to go toward the middle so that her family could see her better. She was feeling guilty. Why wasn't it her instead?

What did she do right?
What if she hadn't?
What did the others do wrong to deserve that?

The formulas just don't work and rarely do they bring anything liberating or inspiring.

Alain de Botton spoke about meritocracy at TEDGlobal 2009. Meritocracy is the idea that if you work hard enough, you can achieve anything you need. Said differently: if you get the pay raise, you earned it; If you don't, you didn't.

Meritocracy is built around faults. It's always your fault. Great if you succeed; horrible if you don't. This is a *new* idea. It was not always this way.

In the Middle Ages, things were a bit different. The poor, or those on the lower rungs of society, were called "less fortunate" because they were seen as not having been visited by fortune. In other words, the poor were described as people whose visits with time and chance had not gone well. So there were fortunate and unfortunate. Botton makes the case that this is no longer true; we now have winners and losers.

Winners have done it right. That's exhilarating.

Losers have not—that can be devastating.

In fact, "it leads to increased rates of suicide. There are more suicides in developed individualistic countries than in any other part of the world. And some of the reason for that is that people take what happens to them extremely personally. They own their success. But they also own their failure."[30]

Because we now own our success and failures arguably more than we ever have, they define us. Determine us. Control us.

Exhilarating and devastating.

What if it's *not* your fault? Rich or poor. Good or bad. Either way.

In this case, an atheist (Botton) and a man described as one who was given wisdom by God (Solomon) happen to agree and that always makes things interesting.

Sometimes there isn't a reason it happened and that's alright. Reality is pain. There is no running from it.

Time and chance happen to us all.

five

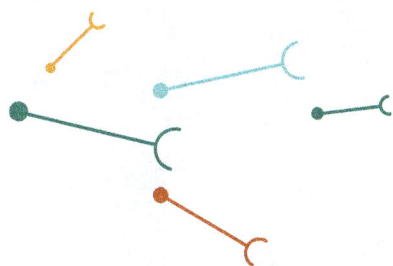

life.

Time and chance, and the pain that comes with them, are here to stay. But, if Solomon is saying anything, he seems to be saying, while there is no place to get to where pain does not live, there is also no place to get to where there is not life, because life is here with us in the same real way.

Of course, some critical questions remain, concerning this "life."

What is it?

What does it mean to say, "I've made it?"

What does it mean to say, "I've got it?"

What, in fact, are *we* trying to do?

What are *you* trying to do?

What is underneath, serving as the foundation for winning the lottery, the kiss in Paris, and the twins?

The question might be one of the most critical in the entire world. If we don't know *what* we're trying to do, then how are we going to know *when* we've done it? If we don't know *what* success looks like, then how are we going to know *when* we're successful?

It's bad enough not getting what we want, but it's worse to have an idea of what we want and finding out that it isn't what we want when we get it.

While working on this chapter I happened to be in Southern California visiting some family. As chance would have it, I happened to spend a morning working on this chapter in a local coffee shop, and as I was typing away an extremely successful person walked into the coffee shop. *Extremely* successful.

Who are the first people that pop into your head? I would love to know some of the names.

> Justin Timberlake?

> Beyoncé?

> Kobe Bryant?

> Kelly Slater?

> Ellen DeGeneres?

Or even the type of person.

> A top executive?

> An owner of a company?

> A well-known chef?

> A celebrity?

> At least a top salesman?

A few years ago, we went on vacation with some friends to a little place east of the Cascades. While there, we visited a couple of wineries.

The first winery was at a man's house. His name was Warren. We had an appointment, and Warren met us with his wife at their front door. Warren, who was in his seventies and happened to have his shirt tucked into his underwear (which were pulled up rather high), walked us back to his garage where the winery was.

I remembered that I couldn't wait to ask my friend why in the world he had booked us here. Warren's garage? There were tools in one corner and wine barrels in another.

Warren showed us his wines. He showed us the wine cellar in the basement of his garage that he had dug by hand. He showed us the wine barrels and talked about how he was one of the first wineries to start in the area. He also told us about his Parkinson's diagnosis.

Eventually, we made our way to his back deck where we sat and tasted his wines. All of Warren's wines are the same price because he doesn't make a wine that is worth less or more than the others. They're all good. We talked about life and wine as Warren sampled each of them with us.

By the time we were done, we bought a few bottles. Unfortunately, Warren didn't take credit cards; Fortunately, he told us to just take the bottles and send him a check in the mail when we got back home.

We did.

After visiting Warren, we went to another winery. It was the "big one" in the area. They had just built a massive tasting room with a fountain, big parking lot, and employees to serve us. We went from tasting wine with two other people to tasting wine with hundreds of people in their beautiful new digs.

This got me asking quite a few questions: Which winery is more successful? The one making more money and selling more bottles of wine or Warren and his back deck (which, I forgot to mention, is also a home for lost cats)?

I guess it depends on what you're going for.

This brings us back to that person who walked into the coffee shop. That successful person. *Extremely* successful.

Did any of these people pop into your head?

> A Jesuit priest?

> A starving artist?

> A high school student?

> A retired firefighter?

> A ski bum?

Why not?

I guess it depends on what you're looking for.

It's amazing how quickly our answers to success—to "making it"—jump to something that has to do with money, power, celebrity, or grand achievements of some kind and never to a guy in his seventies making some wine in a garage (with his cats in the background) and drinking it with the people who come by.

What *are* we looking for? One would think that religions like Christianity would help to answer the question, but, arguably, most versions of it have only confused us more.

> Sometimes it's money. God will bless you if you give. Give more money to the church or charities or whatever else, and you'll receive. Because that's the final goal.

> Sometimes it's the lack of money, or poverty. God wants you to live with nothing. Give away all you have and be with the poor. It still revolves around amounts of money, but less is better, and none is best.

> Sometimes it's education or wisdom. Learn, understand, have answers for people and their problems. And your problems.

> Sometimes it's family or legacy or marriage. Nothing is more important than family, we say. Be a good parent, be a good sibling, be a good husband or a good wife, leave something beautiful behind that lasts.

> Sometimes it's evangelism. Spread the "gospel." Convert people. Get them on board. Have them sign on the dotted line. Like a sales person, the more you get, the more successful you are in the eyes of "the boss."

> Sometimes it's being happy.

> Sometimes it's being holy and happiness isn't even a part of it because, as it's said, God wants you to be holy, not happy.

Sometimes it's helping people.

Sometimes it's loving people and/or loving God.

Sometimes it's just surviving this crazy world in whatever way you can—it really doesn't matter—and getting to Heaven because that's where the success really is.

Not to say that all, or any, of these are bad or wrong or not worth giving some thought to, but what if it's not any of these?

Then what is it?

While Christianity has contributed to the confusion, it's hardly as though Christianity can be the main recipient of blame. No one else seems to be offering up any great answers either. Alain de Botton has dedicated an entire TED Talk to the idea of success, its complexity, and the ridiculousness of many of the answers,[31] and in the end says that we must come up with our own ideas of it.

This *is* a question for all of us.

What does success look like? What is the good stuff?

What is "life?" For me?

Agassi was 31 at the time. He was coming out of drug use, a failed marriage, playing bad tennis, hating tennis, and hating himself. But he came back. He won the Australian Open in one of the most lopsided victories ever, which was also his eighth Grand Slam. He was the oldest person in 31 years to win a Grand Slam tournament. He was back, maybe better than ever. And he writes:

> As they hand me the trophy, I tell the crowd: There's not a single day that's guaranteed to us, and certainly days like this are very rare.
>
> Someone says later that I sounded as if I'd had a near-death experience.

> More like a near-life experience. It's how a person talks when he almost didn't live.[32]

My brother- and sister-in-law have an exchange student from Spain who is living with them right now. She's an awesome girl, just getting a grasp on English. Show her the above paragraph and you will see a confused expression.

Someone who is alive is saying I almost didn't live? It's hard enough for us to understand even if English is our first language.

And yet.

It makes so much sense, it hits us in those places of emotion and soul that we don't tap into very often, but when we do, they strike truth.

I almost didn't live.

The world is full of dead people. They are everywhere. Everything breathes, but not everything lives.

High schools are as filled with them as are nursing homes. It has nothing to do with age.

Penthouse suites around the world are filled with them as are homeless shelters. It has nothing to do with money.

Strip clubs and casinos, arenas and office buildings, churches and mosques are filled with them. It has nothing to do with religion.

It is the ultimate definition of being successful: being alive. Not just breathing and walking and talking, but being alive.

Awake.

Aware.

Present.

> "Wouldn't it be awful to die and never again see or hear or love or move?"

"You find that awful?" said the Master. "But that's how most people are even before they die."[33]

This is the life we are talking about: to see and hear and love and move while we're breathing. There might be pain, sure, but there is also *living* in the truest sense of the word. That is the success that we're talking about, and the reality that Solomon says is here is more plentiful and as real as any pain.

In fact, sometimes it's right there in the middle of it.

six

back to pain.

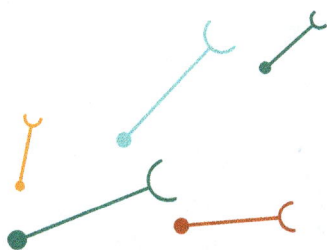

A certain beauty finds itself in the dark.

What an exquisite use of words.

I want to be careful because sayings can be cute and trite and I don't mean for this saying to be either one. If someone said something like that after my wife was just killed in a random way, I would not find it amusing or even be willing to hear it.

And, yet, there is something sacredly true about the words. There is something that strikes us with power and rawness and energy. They are not simple or trite words, but inspiring and cleansing words.

They have been said in many other ways by people who have earned the right and are much more capable than me. So I will let them speak for a moment.

André Agassi, in the middle of one of his worst moments, found comfort in the words of C.S. Lewis who had lost his wife to illness:

> Pain is God's megaphone to rouse a deaf world. He tells them: We are like blocks of stone ... [T]he blows of His chisel, which hurt us so much, are what make us perfect.[34]

Pain makes us perfect?

Michael J. Fox, who has suffered through the pain of Parkinson's disease, said this in his memoir:

> If you were to rush into this room right now and announce that you had struck a deal—with God, Allah, Buddha, Christ, Krishna, Bill Gates, whomever—in which the ten years since my diagnosis could be magically taken away, traded in for ten more years as

the person I was before—I would, without a moment's hesitation, tell you to take a hike.[35]

He wouldn't trade his Parkinson's for a life without it? "Take a hike?"

When I read *A Severe Mercy* a few years ago, I found myself bawling like a baby in my bed while my wife looked over at me wondering if I was alright. I have never been moved by any story like I was by the amazing story of a man, the love of his life, and her death. Stunning. And the man who lost his wife writes this about himself:

> But in the books again, great joy through love always seemed to go hand in hand with frightful pain. Still, he thought, looking out across the meadow, still, the joy would be worth the pain—if indeed, they went together. If there were a choice—and he suspected there was—a choice between, on the one hand, the heights and the depths and, on the other hand, some sort of safe, cautious middle way, he, for one, here and now chose the heights and the depths.
>
> Since then the years have gone by and he—had he not had what he chose that day in the meadow? He had had the love. And the joy—what joy it had been! And the sorrow. He had had—was having—all the sorrow there was. And yet, the joy was worth the pain. Even now he re-affirmed that long-past choice.[36]

"The joy was worth the pain?" But his pain was enough to give me pain just reading about it years later. I can't imagine what the pain he experienced actually felt like.

Was it really worth it? Really?

In the fictional, and future, age of *Brave New World*, pain has been eradicated, which brings up an entirely new set of thoughts around whether that's something any of us would *really* want.

Pleasure reigns supreme. In one of the most powerful scenes of the book, a "savage," who has grown up in a world where pain does still exist, finds himself face to face with Mustapha Mond, one of the government officials responsible for removing pain. They have this conversation:

> "What you need," the Savage went on, "is something with tears for a change. Nothing costs enough here.
>
> "But I don't want comfort. I want God, I want poetry, I want real danger, I want freedom, I want goodness. I want sin."
>
> "In fact," said Mustapha Mond, "you're claiming the right to be unhappy."
>
> "All right then," said the Savage defiantly, "I'm claiming the right to be unhappy.
>
> "Not to mention the right to grow old and ugly and impotent; the right to have syphilis and cancer; the right to have too little to eat; the right to be lousy; the right to live in constant apprehension of what may happen tomorrow; the right to catch typhoid; the right to be tortured by unspeakable pains of every kind."
>
> There was a long silence. "I claim them all," said the Savage at last.[37]

"Nothing costs enough." Three words you could ponder for a long time. What would things mean without the cost and contrast of pain? Even in my own life, I have thought about all of the costs associated with the things I care most about.

My marriage. My kids. My job. My faith. My friends. Running. Creating. They are some of the most precious things to me, and, yet, they are precious because of their cost—because of their pain. They are not a pain, in any way, but they have cost me, of course.

These are small pains, compared to what some go through. Yet, there *is* something that pain and darkness brings us—something beautiful that nothing else can. There is no denying it.

All the way to death?

Flight came out in 2012 and received Academy Award nominations for Best Original Screenplay and Best Actor. It's the story of Whip Whitaker, a pilot and alcoholic who heroically saves a plane. At, perhaps, the most powerful moment of the movie, Whip finds himself in a hospital with a terminal cancer patient who says this:

> It's a trip . . . they think because I'm close to the other side I got some sort of power or wisdom—like I got all the answers. I don't know, maybe I do. Death gives you perspective. It all makes sense somehow.
>
> I just can't get over how beautiful you are . . .
>
> My family just flew in from Utah. You know it's bad when they start flying in. This is a trip 'cause every morning is special now. I'm grateful of that. I wish I could bottle this feeling that I have about how beautiful every last breath of life is.

These are words from a movie, but they are more than fiction. They reek of authenticity written by someone who knows . . . who has experienced it . . . and we sense them to be true.

"Death gives you perspective. I wish I could bottle up this feeling that I have about how beautiful every last breath of life is."

Such hauntingly beautiful words about success and pain.

Ric Elias, who was on US Airways Flight 1549 when it landed in the Hudson said: " . . . as we're coming down, I had a sense of, wow, dying is not scary. It's almost like we've been preparing for it our whole lives."

He also said his life will never be the same again from what he learned.[38] The pain was worth it.

Solomon writes:

> *It is better to go to a house of mourning than to go to a house of feasting, for death is the destiny of everyone; the living should take this to heart.*

Frustration is better than laughter, because a sad face is good for the heart. The heart of the wise is in the house of mourning, but the heart of fools is in the house of pleasure.[39]

Read that one more time.

Maybe it's more than just saying time and chance and pain and darkness are here just as much as life. Maybe it's saying we shouldn't be as frightened of the pain as we often are. Maybe it's saying we should not only be alright with going to a funeral, but look forward to it, because it reminds us of the life we should be living—and that alone is a beauty worth finding.

That is success.

What if a sad face really is good for the heart? What if the heart of the wise really does stay in the house of mourning and the heart of fools really does stay in the house of pleasure?

If that were true, what would it mean? How would it affect the way we live? How would it affect the way we look at circumstances? How would it change the actual appearance of the circumstances?

Maybe we could say it this way—about the first truth of living on the island: There is time, there is chance, there is pain, there is darkness, there is beauty, there are people who are alive, and there are people who are living, and not only are we surrounded by all of them, but they are inexorably tied together in a myriad of ways. Maybe it's time we stop trying to untie a knot we may not actually even want to untie and stop trying to understand how they each work and start understanding how to live in the midst of all of them?

seven

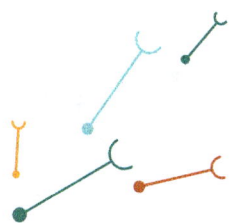

mystery.

As you do not know the path of the wind, or how the body is formed in a mother's womb, so you cannot understand the work of God, the Maker of all things.[40]

Sometimes she feels like a cool kiss on the cheek and other times like a hot slap in the face. I hate her and I love her. Sometimes she's pushing with a pleasant nudge and other times she's forcing me back, like a trainer with full resistance. So I have to run harder.

I don't know if she gets angry, but it feels like she does when she comes onto our deck and wreaks her havoc, overturning umbrellas and furniture and tablecloths. And that's the least of her destruction—she'll uproot trees and tear off roofs.

And, yet, she'll push a boat across waves and bring a smile to any child who holds onto a piece of string and watches her kick around the kite on the other end, high up in the sky.

She's as strong as they come. Give her enough time and she'll shape rock. We sing her praises when she blows out clouds of toxins from a fertilizer plant explosion, and we curse her when she wreaks havoc on a small town in Oklahoma, ripping it apart like a toddler does to her Legos.

As much as she's in our life, and as much as we use her to our advantage—and watch her take advantage of us, we don't really have much control over her. We can harvest her, we can redirect her, we can bask in her relief, we can beg her to leave, we can block her and hide from her, but we can't *stop* her.

She's always there in some form or another.

Sometimes with smiles and laughter and sometimes with sweat and trepidation. Sure, we can *explain* her.

Wind is caused by air flowing from high pressure to low pressure. The Earth's rotation prevents that flow from being direct, but deflects it side to side (right in the Northern Hemisphere and left in the Southern), so wind flows around the high and low pressure areas.[41]

And, yet, I don't know . . . the words just don't do much for a mystery like her.

I held him and stared. If you haven't held a human being who has only been breathing air for less time than it takes to watch a movie, you haven't yet lived. Find a baby. There's something astounding, magical and miraculous.

The little chest heaving up and down, the heart racing, the feet squirming, the eyes darting around, the finger that wraps around your own. The nostrils, the toenails, and that umbilical cord that was providing life for it, just hours ago. Even if you just stare, you can't help but marvel.

Of course we can *explain* him.

The process of fertilization involves a sperm fusing with an ovum. The most common sequence begins with ejaculation during copulation, follows with ovulation, and finishes with fertilization. Upon encountering the ovum, the acrosome of the sperm produces enzymes which allow it to burrow through the outer jelly coat of the egg. The sperm plasma then fuses with the egg's plasma membrane, the sperm head disconnects from its flagellum and the egg travels down the Fallopian tube to reach the uterus.[42]

Ovum, sequence, acrosome, and plasma membrane help us to understand a mystery like him?

The mathematician Alexander Tsiaras, an Associate Professor of Medicine and Chief of Scientific Visualization at Yale University in the Department of Medicine (Is that a title or what!? Imagine that on a business card.) used new scanning technology to look at the development of a fetus from conception to birth. He said this about what he had learned:

The magic of the mechanisms inside each genetic structure saying exactly where that nerve cell should go—the complexity of these mathematical models of how these things are indeed done are beyond human comprehension.

Even though I am a mathematician, I look at this with marvel of how do these instruction sets not make these mistakes as they build what is us? It's a mystery, it's magic, it's divinity.[43]

So, a mathematician in 2013 has tracked every aspect of the forming of a human and calls it "a mystery" and "magic?"

When Jesus was walking around and talking to people, including a particular religious leader of the day named Nicodemus, he used two words to describe what this new perspective, this new way of being alive, looked like: wind and birth.[44] Jesus borrowed two things that Solomon used to illustrate mystery and he used both of them to describe what he was bringing to town.

In other words, the way Jesus was talking about looking at things involved a lot of mystery. A whole lot.

Somehow the people, who claimed to follow Jesus, took cues from "born again" and "wind" and ran with them. And, it seems, they ran with them far enough to make them fit into a nice, little comic strip, or a few words of a prayer, or five bars of color, or a "salvation bracelet,"[45] or, at least, a quick 15-minute "come to Jesus" sermon . . . all of which are about as far from mysterious as one can get.

I don't think religious people are alone in running from mystery whenever we can. Most of us don't really like. Some of my friends promise me that science will eventually have an answer for everything. And who knows, maybe it will?

But, do we *really* want answers for everything?

According to one of the most brilliant scientists to ever live, Einstein, maybe not.

"The most beautiful emotion we can experience is the mysterious. It is the power of all true art and science. He to whom this emotion is a stranger, who can no longer pause to wonder and stand rapt in awe, is as good as dead."[46]

The power of all true art and science and the most beautiful emotion we can experience?

Do we *really* want to know all the answers and lose that?

We seem to think we do. We, generally crave the 10 steps to happiness, 12 methods to freedom, 7 techniques to success, and 3 facts about money. We buy books, we listen to speakers, and we often go to the Bible—or whatever holy book we follow—or science to find our answers.

But Solomon keeps saying they are not there—not *that* formula and not *those* answers. Science, I would argue, seems to be saying the same thing: the more we uncover in regard to the basic functions of the universe (the quantum world has blown most of the old Newtonian rules out of the water),[47] the more we realize it's bathed in randomness and mystery and empty space.

In 1927, Heisenberg made his famous statement: We cannot know, as a matter of principle, the present in all of its details because an electron cannot "know" where it is and where it is going at the same time.[48]

In other words, we can't even truly know the present because the basic building blocks of the present don't know it themselves.

It's seems about as likely that science will never have mystery as it it is that we will one day prove God exists. Not very.

Jesus seemed to have said the same thing, which is probably why people struggled—and still struggle today—with what he said. And often the more religious we are, the more we struggle. We're threatened by what we can't control, just like we're threatened by the wind. We're uncomfortable with transformations that are magical, just like the birth of a baby. We don't like the part of God that comes and goes, and does not fit into our structured beliefs and theologies.

So, we build golden cows. We don't want a God we can't control.

But this mystery of the universe seems to be a theme among the sacred and secular, the spiritual and scientific. If we're going to talk about a way to handle the darkness and the beauty, we're going to have to find a way to handle mystery and magic and a lack of control and understanding. As frustrating as "I don't know" can be, they might also be some of the most liberating and beautiful words that exist.

We don't *have* to keep trying to always "know." If we don't have to have all the answers and the correct formulas, maybe we can begin to discover and create and fully live again?

Trying to have the answers is the thing that often clogs our capacity to live.

Which brings us back to Solomon.

> *Ship your grain across the sea; after many days you may receive a return. Invest in seven ventures, yes, in eight; you do not know what disaster may come upon the land. If clouds are full of water, they pour rain on the earth. Whether a tree falls to the south or to the north, in the place where it falls, there it will lie. Whoever watches the wind will not plant; whoever looks at the clouds will not reap.*[49]

Have you ever met someone who spends so much time trying to figure how to know when it's going to rain that they never spend any time actually planting something that the rain might benefit?

Or enjoying the rain when it comes?

Have you ever met someone who spends so much time determining how to deduce and understand the wind and to know when it will come and from what direction that they never throw the seed down for fear that the wind will carry the seed to the wrong spot?

Or think to create a windmill?

Or just fly a kite?

Have you ever met someone who is so enamored with understanding God and the Bible and theology and doctrine that they never actually live the life the Bible tells stories about and that God has given them?

At some point, we don't understand. At some point, it just doesn't work. At some point, it's no use. And how much time do we waste in trying to understand and make it work when we could just be living?

So Solomon says to ship our grains across the seas. It's time to go for it. What else is there to do? We can no longer sit around and wait until there is no risk, no fear, no likelihood of time and chance getting it wrong.

> No one can comprehend what goes on under the sun. Despite all their efforts to search it out, no one can discover its meaning. Even if the wise claim they know, they cannot really comprehend it.[50]

We can ask: "What's the point of all of this?" or we can stop trying to figure it all out and go plant some crops and *live*.

I was flying out of Seattle recently. Just after takeoff, the plane shot through a low layer of clouds and Mount Rainier was right outside the opposite side's window. This massive, snowcapped mountain was bathed in enough sunlight for everyone on that side of the plane to let out an orchestrated . . .

"Whoa."

Later I was traveling down the highway at about 65 mph. A car went flying by in an attempt to pass me and a car that was a decent distance ahead. As the car went roaring by, I saw another car coming toward us, and I wondered if he was going to go for it. He did. And he made it. But not before my heart raced, and I stared wide-eyed at my wife, and we said, together:

"Whoa."

There's a great YouTube video of a guy named Danny MacAskill. He rides a bike on top of fences, on roofs, on sidewalks . . . pretty much anywhere you can imagine a bicycle being ridden in a city as well as places you can't imagine. If you watch it with others, it's one of those videos where people look at each other and pull back from the screen saying "whaaaaaat" and there are yells and shouts of pure wonder. We showed it at our church and everyone kept repeating . . .

"Whoa."

There's great pleasure in it. Just sitting there and saying . . .

"Whoa."

When whoa comes, we don't ask ourselves . . .

Why am I seeing this mountain?

What does it mean?

How this metal tube is able to get to 14,000 feet so fast, and why the sun is reflecting off the snow?

Is the universe trying to tell me something?

How did the car barely miss us?

Why did he ride on that fence?

Why was I able to see this?

Is it a sign of something else?

No, we just say . . .

"Whoa."

It's inspiration and wonder . . . unadulterated mystery in its most distilled form. And sometimes *that* is the point. Just to sit and bask in the awe.

There's a story about Jesus. Most people have heard the story in some form or another. It's evening and the guys that have been following Jesus around are in a boat on the shore of a lake.[51] They wait around for

Jesus for awhile, but he doesn't show up so they decide to leave and head toward the other side of the lake without him.

On their way, the winds start to kick up and the waters start to get pretty rough. They've rowed three or four miles—which is a pretty good distance—and it's starting to approach dawn. It's possible they have been rowing all night.

They're exhausted and drained and sick of rowing when they see what they think is a ghost on the water—an apparition. (Apparently it's easier to believe in ghosts walking on water rather than people.) Eventually, however, they find out it's Jesus.

This is interesting. Why is Jesus walking on water? Does he do this for fun? Is this how he usually gets around? Is he trying to impress them? One of the accounts of the story says that Jesus was going to pass them by, without them even seeing him.

There may *not* have been a point to this whole thing.

But they do see him and they are freaked out. What is he doing on the water? Like that? And Jesus says, "Don't be afraid; it's me." They then take him into the boat and the winds calm down.

There are some other parts to the story but, interestingly, that's all there is in John's account. That's *all* to his story. They're on a boat, and Jesus walks out onto the water to meet them. Story over. There are no sermons from Jesus on the other side. No sermons about getting through the storms of life or about rowing hard enough to get to where we need to get to or about looking to Jesus when life gets hard.

They don't hear a point or a message or a doctrine or a theology or a formula to any of this.

They don't hear any answers.

When I imagine those disciples sitting around later that evening and talking about what they had seen, I don't imagine them trying to deduce what it meant or why they were shown that or what Jesus was trying to tell them. I imagine them sitting around a fire and saying . . .

"Whoa. That was pretty cool."

Imagine if they had been so focused on rowing and afraid of what the storm would do, or wouldn't do, and had never looked up. An opportunity to say "whoa" would have passed them right by. I once heard an astronomer talk about the number of people who never stop to look up at the sky to see the stars at night. They miss out on an opportunity.

Why is that?

The story goes on to say that other people heard about Jesus from this whole walking on water thing. They were apparently moved by an inspiring story, without needing to understand it, just like we all are today. Whoa was as contagious then as it is now.

When and how did we manage to take the "whoa" out of this whole thing?

Have you ever stood in front of a great painting?

Have you ever listened to an amazing song?

Have you ever watched a movie and stayed in the chair during the credits because you didn't want it to be over?

"Whoa."

This is what great art does. It moves us. It speaks to us. We don't have to ask why, or what does it all mean, or what am I supposed to take from it.

We enjoy it because we already know.

At times we're just supposed to be blasted with a wave of wonder, stunned with beauty, saturated with awe, and we don't have anything else to do but to take it all in and enjoy it. Because that is how this world and this God operate, and when we begin to live in a world like that, we might actually start to be more alive. Research carried out at Stanford University by Melanie Rudd has shown that a sense of awe "expands people's perceptions of time, enhances feelings of well-being, and even causes people to behave more altruistically and less materialistically."[52]

Others have said that wonder is what unites three of the greatest human institutions: science, religion, and art.[53]

Why do we seem to intent at taking the wonder out of all of them?

There are many points that can be taken from the creation poem of the Bible. But there is one I never realized until recently. And it might be the most powerful.

The poem goes from man, woman, and everything good to man, woman, and everything not so good. If we don't get distracted by the talking snakes and fruit, we see something pretty astounding.

The act that starts things moving from good to not good is the temptation of knowledge: an insistence on knowing. *That's* where everything started to get messed up.[54]

The desire to know destroyed that garden.

"Whoa."

> "To accept everything is an exercise, to understand everything a strain. The poet only desires exaltation and expansion, a world to stretch himself in. The poet only asks to get his head into the heavens. It is the logician who seeks to get the heavens into his head. And it is his head that splits."[55]

"Whoa."

Too many of us are running around with headaches these days, especially religious people. Too many of us are trying to find all the answers and missing out on the wonder of mystery.

Maybe we could say this about the truths of living on the island: There is time, there is chance, there is pain, there is darkness, there is beauty, there are people who are alive and there are people who are living, and not only are we surrounded by all of them, but they are inexorably and mysteriously tied together in a myriad of unknown ways. Maybe it's time we stop trying to untie a knot we may not actually even want to untie and stop trying to understand how they each work and start appreciating the whoas and wonders and awe and mystery that surround them, and us, each and every moment?

eight

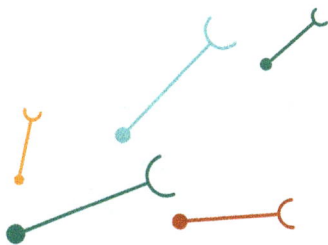

stop.

Brené Brown writes: "We are a culture of people who've bought into the idea that if we stay busy enough, the truth of our lives won't catch up with us."[56]

Born into a state of perpetual motion . . . just like the baby caribou.

When does the perpetual motion stop?

If we're going to *get* anywhere, then we're going to have to stop at some point.

So, when do we?

> Stop posting pictures on Instagram?
>
> Stop reading everyone's opinions on Facebook?
>
> Stop caring about what everyone else is doing?
>
> Stop building?
>
> Stop running?
>
> Stop exercising?
>
> Stop creating clubs?
>
> Stop interviewing?
>
> Stop planning?
>
> Stop trying to figure out the answers that will make it all work?
>
> Stop filling our life with activity?

Stop thinking?

Stop rowing the boat to that island?

Stop reading new books with new information? (It's possible you should even put this book down for a little while.)

I'm admittedly an impatient person. As a result, I have fights with dresser and drawers. I'm talking about the ones where the hammers and pans get stuck in. You know the one. You can't open the drawer, because the hammer or pan is lodged in there just perfectly and the fact that you can't open the drawer gets you yanking on the drawer even harder which just gets the hammer or pan stuck even more stuck.

My daughter once had a dresser that had been in the family for way too long and, as a result, it didn't work right. It was off-center and crooked and the bottom of the drawer would fall apart because the glue and nails no longer held, and it wouldn't open. I would get in all-out fights with this thing while trying to get my daughter's pink pajamas out of it.

In every one of these situations, the only way to actually open the drawer and get what we're looking for, is to stop the antics and slowly push the drawer in the opposite direction of where we actually want it to go. Then we can reach into that little crack and push down the hammer or the pan, or lift the bottom of the drawer and gently open it.

So many of us are railing on dressers and trying to get drawers to open and filling our lives with activity, rowing, putting up sails, searching for answers, and becoming exhausted.

Maybe it's time we stop and do the opposite of what we think we're supposed to. Maybe it's time to calm down and breathe again—to listen and uncover the best way to actually move forward.

Which often starts with stopping. There are times the only way to move forward is to do the one thing that seems more absurd than any other . . . to stop trying.

That Hebrew creation poem[57] says that God stopped. Imagine that for a second: God stopping to take a break. Does your view of God ever have God stopping? Have you ever thought of a God who stops to listen to a song or to watch a sunset or to smell a summer rain? The Hebrew creation poem has God doing exactly that.

This God stops to enjoy and bask for a moment in the awe and wonder and good of creation.

And a song for the universe is established. This song is a beautiful, poetic, majestic melody, and it involves something very particular and necessary built into the foundation of any good song: rhythm. And for something to be a rhythm, it has to have times of stopping; otherwise, it's just a hum. And a hum is cool, but it's not what keeps a song going at the right pace.

Stopping is what keeps us *going* at the right pace. To go in the melodic way we have to stop.

Anyone who has ever been on a vacation knows this. If you've traveled to a tropical paradise, you know it even more. It's called "island time" for a reason. It's almost as if time stops. The things that were thought important are not. People are late because time is not the dictator it is in other parts of the world. They are late because it's okay to be late.

I have a friend who spent about six months in Fiji. She told me she never realized how fast she walked and that she had to learn to "walk slow."

When we go to these places with island time, we stop. And it feels tremendous. We slow down. And it's rejuvenating.

A few months ago, my wife and I were in Kauai. We sat on a beach for four hours and stared at water, at a sunset, at people, at a sea turtle that had stopped (because everything in nature stops), and we didn't look at a phone, an iPad, or even a book.

We just sat there. We weren't bored or anxious; we were calm and at peace.

Which makes one ask: If it's so good to stop, then why do we have such trouble doing it? Especially in the fast-paced West?

Maybe it's because some of us view stopping as being weak. We've all heard that real men don't stop and that real women have too much work to do and that none of us "have time for that".

We're all "too busy." What kind of a world would we have if we all stopped? Can you imagine the chaos that would ensue? We just can't!

Stopping is what keeps us *going* at the right pace. To work in the melodic way we have to stop.

This is not about stopping. It's about *going* in a more true and healthy way. This is not about silence. This is about a song. This is about rhythm and silence in a ratio that creates something bigger than both.

That Hebrew creation poem established a rhythm with six days of work and one day of rest. The people who followed the God of that poem established a similar pattern in most everything they did.

Rest for a day. Create for six.

Rest for a day. Create for six.

Grow crops for six years. Let the land rest for one.

Earn for six. Spread the wealth on the seventh.

Rhythm. Work and rest. Create and rest. Go and stop.

But maybe the real reason that we don't like to stop relates to control. When we stop, we also let go of control and we never like to let go of control.

> What if someone else does something while I'm not doing anything?

> What if the whole company falls apart without me?

> What if someone beats me to it?

What if I miss something from God?

What if I mess up?

What if I break my habit?

What if?

Then what?

This is called vulnerability. Let it happen. Though our world has found a way to look down on being vulnerable it's in the vulnerability and in the stopping where joy, creativity, and love are born. They require the rhythm. They require the letting go.

They also start when you stop.[58]

Missing joy? Missing creativity? Missing love?
When was the last time you stopped?

It's hard to stop metaphorically, spiritually, emotionally, mentally, or any other way if we don't begin by stopping physically. So put down the phone, make a list of all the things you are saying yes to already, plan a night on the calendar where you don't do anything (you can still tell people you are busy) and stop.

See

how

good

it

feels?

Try it now.

Just

breathe.

Listen.

To the sounds around you.

Shhh . . .

Just

listen . . .

When

was

the
       last
            time
                you
                    saw
                        God?

When

was

the
       last
            time
                you
                    stopped to look at the stars?

Sometimes it starts right there.

nine

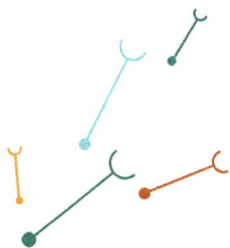

let god go.

Remember that golden cow? The one that the followers of the "one true God" built because they were tired of waiting for God?

We are still building them. But our cows look a little different because our culture looks a little different. Gods aren't made of our jewelry anymore. We've evolved. Our gods are made of theologies and doctrines and answers instead. But the reasoning is the same.

We are tired of waiting. Which really means we're tired of the lack of control. If God is big and mysterious and complex and more like wind and newborns than a textbook, we will put effort into reining that God in. To control that God a little more. To have something tangible that we can worship.

Maybe we haven't evolved much.

We're still spending inordinate amounts of time to make God small. If, the logic goes, God is beyond our ideas, then that God cannot work for us. And if that God does not work for us, then how will that God ever give us what we're supposed to get or want to get?

What use is *that* God?

What use is a God that is more like a wild lion when we want a house cat that we can pet and feed and that will never run far from home or threaten to overtake us?

What use is a God that moves like wind and birth, with awe and mystery, when we want that vending machine that we can put in an if and pick out a then?

And so we begin to manipulate the gods, manipulate religion, manipulate theology to serve . . . us.

"Thus, Solomon and Saint Paul both insisted on the largeness and the at-largeness of God, setting him free, so to speak, from ideas about Him. He is not to be fenced in, under human control, like some domestic creature; He is the wildest being in existence. The presence of His spirit in us is our wildness, our oneness with the wilderness of Creation."[59]

Think about those words for a second.

Set God free from the ideas about Him.

Or her.

Or it.

Or them.

(The Bible describes God with all of those words not to mention words like spirit, light, water, wind, fire, a shepherd, a king, a bush on fire, love, a Father, a nursing mother, a judge, a potter, a rock, a warrior, a friend, a lawgiver, and as Jesus.)

How can God be a mother and a father, a rock and a bush on fire, water and wind?

How can God be a her and a him and a them?

When was the last time you thought of God as the wildest being in existence?

Some of us simply need to let God out of the psychological fences in our brain and faiths and back into the open spaces of the universe to roam free and wild again. Some of us need to stop trying to make God work for us and start seeing the wildness of the God that actually exists in reality.

St. Thomas Aquinas famously said, "The highest form of the knowledge of God is to know that one does not know . . ."[60]

When was the last time you heard a pastor say that the best God you can get to know is a God that you *know* you *cannot* know?

At the beginning of *Toy Story 3* is a fantastic short film called *Day and Night*. During the short, the following lines are recited from a 1970s lecture:

> "Fear of the unknown. They are afraid of new ideas. They are loaded with prejudices, not based upon anything in reality, but based on . . . if something is new, I reject it immediately because it's frightening to me. What they do instead is just stay with the familiar. You know, to me, the most beautiful things in all the universe, are the most mysterious."[61]

If God is unknown, if Jesus is bringing something revolutionary and new, if so much of our concepts are not based on reality . . .

Is it any wonder that so many fail to see God? Even in church? It's a very dangerous thing to stay with the familiar God and reject everything else because the new ideas are too frightening.

Or because we get what we want with the old ideas.

Look at history. Look at those who killed Jesus.

Stop,
set God free,
let go of what you want,
and enter into the beautiful mystery that *is.* God.

ten

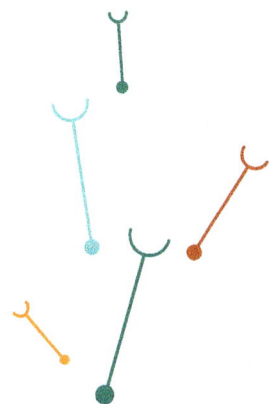

let the trolls go.

It was a weird week. It was rainy. I had a fever blister and I hate fever blisters. (Fever blisters have this way of really getting under my skin in a way something that small just shouldn't.) I was working on a talk that was not coming together and it was becoming more frustrating and almost panic-inducing. *What if I just don't have anything to say anymore?* The weirdness was in the air. It was almost suffocating, borderline depressing.

I went on a run, assuming that the exercise would shake off the weirdness like it usually does. But it didn't. Everything was off. I started trying to figure out why I was really off. What was behind it all?

While running, I began to think about fear. My fears. The fears about health, about age, about skills, about creativity or the lack of it, the fears for my wife and kids, the fears for our church, the fears of the future, the fears that are always swirling around money. The ifs and thens that walk through life with us like little annoying trolls, always reminding us of all the things that could go wrong—are likely to go wrong—and how miserable our life is about to become.

The fears were getting under my skin in a way that worst-case imagining should not. But that's exactly what fear does. Just like a fever blister. So I had had enough. I started talking out loud, and I looked up at the cloudy skies and said, "F--- you, fear!"

The more I said it, the louder it got until I was eventually yelling above the music in my headphones. If people drove by and saw me, they were probably struck with their own fear for my mental state *and* ability to be a pastor.

Then I started to cry. Big tears. Tears that would have embarrassed me if anyone had seen me. I was a complete wreck. Yelling out at the air and crying, and all because of thoughts about things that had not happened, but *could*.

Every human being has them. Some do better at masking them; some do better at pretending they aren't there; some do better at dealing with them; and some do better at telling them to f--- off because there is too much life to live.

But we all deal with that little troll who looks up at us with those red eyes and reminds us of the . . .

Fear of not being important.
Fear of not being elevated.
Fear of not being treasured.
Fear of being abandoned.
Fear of not being noticed.
Fear of not having enough money.
Fear of being alone.
Fear of not being loved.
Fear of cancer or disease.
Fear of criticism.
Fear of failing.
Fear of authority.
Fear of offending God.
Fear of not having enough fear.
Fear of other groups.
Fear of change.
Fear of hell.
Fear of being unworthy.
Fear of interpreting the Bible incorrectly.
Fear of bad theology.
Fear of doubt.
Fear of the unknown.
Fear of being wrong.
Fear of death.

And the list could go on all day. They live deep in our souls. They are impossible to satisfy. As soon as one fear is gone, we fear what will happen if the fear returns or if we lose the thing that sent the fear away.

If I *get* money, the fear of never having enough money transforms into the fear of *losing* the money that I've got. If I *find* love, the fear of never being alone becomes the fear of *losing* the person that makes me feel loved. And on and on it goes . . . the troll always wins.

We can never win.

And these fears distract us. They paralyze us. They take over and destroy our ability to be creative, to take risks, to innovate because we become afraid that we *might* fail, or it *might* not work, or we *could* be wrong . . . and then what *would* happen?

Just more fears fill in the empty spaces. We never run out of them.

Here are some crazy numbers:

> The United States spends 60 billion dollars a year to prevent terrorism.

> International terrorism kills an average of about 379 people a year worldwide.

> Malaria kills 1 million children a year.

> Most experts say it would cost around 2 to 3 billion dollars a year to completely control malaria.

So, even though malaria will kill 67 times more people each year than terrorism, the United States will spend 20 times more money each year fighting terrorism than it would take to remove malaria from the globe.[62]

The United States spends 67 times more money every year on preventing 379 potential deaths than saving the lives of 1 million. Guaranteed.

Don't let the politics blind you to the main point. This is not about whether or not we should put resources into terrorism. Of course, terrorism is a hideous evil and any life lost is a life that should be grieved and seen as a tragedy. Of course, the amount of money spent to prevent terrorism actually does prevent it.

But. Do those numbers *really* make sense? Where do they come from?

When was the last time you were afraid, or told to be afraid, of malaria? When was the last time you were afraid, or told to be afraid, of a terrorist attack?

Fear determines, controls, and conducts *so* much of what we do.

So religion came up with an answer to these fears. A way to save us from these trolls and their incessant distraction and mocking. Religion invited a formula that goes something like this:

> Fear not: trust in God and He will see that none of the things you fear will happen to you.[63]

The *classic* if and then: *If* you trust in God enough, *then* the fears will go away. This kind of statement has been called illusory religion. False religion. Illusions are things which do not exist and statements or religions that go along with them simply do not exist.

Idols. Formulas. Perpetual cycles. It's what Solomon has been telling us. Vapors and mist. Meaningless.

Walter White is the main character on the television show *Breaking Bad*. The premise of the show is that Walter, a disillusioned high school chemistry teacher, is diagnosed with terminal lung cancer and begins to sell drugs to secure some kind of future for his family. Good one, right?

In Season 2, Walter says the following to his brother-in-law, Hank, in a beautiful scene:

> I have spent my whole life scared. Frightened of things that could happen, might happen, might not happen. 50 years I spent like that. Finding myself awake at three in the morning. But you know what? Ever since my diagnosis I sleep just fine. I came to realize it's that fear that's the worst of it. That's the real enemy.

Band of Brothers is the HBO mini-series that chronicles Easy Company of the US 101st Airborne division during World War II. Another amazing piece of storytelling and production. At one point, the character Lt. Spiers finds himself talking to a younger soldier, Blithe, who had frozen up during the invasion of Normandy. They have the following conversation:

> Blithe: Lt., sir, when I landed on D-Day I found myself in a ditch all by myself. I fell asleep. I think it was air sickness. When I woke up I didn't really try to find my unit to fight . . . just . . . I just kinda stayed put.

Spiers: You know why you hid in that ditch, Blithe?

Blithe: I was scared.

Spiers: We're all scared. You hid in that ditch because you think there is still hope. But, Blithe, the only hope you have is to accept the fact you're already dead, and the sooner you accept that the sooner you'll be able to function as a solider is supposed to function.

Powerful statements. The fear is the worst of it. Once you deal with them you can start to live and function.

Remember those lines from Solomon?

> It is better to go to a house of mourning than to go to a house of feasting, for death is the destiny of everyone; the living should take this to heart.

> Frustration is better than laughter, because a sad face is good for the heart. The heart of the wise is in the house of mourning, but the heart of fools is in the house of pleasure.[64]

At some point, we have to stop. We have to stop being paralyzed by fear; we have to stop worrying that they *might* come true, and we have to start living the way we are supposed to live.

At some point.

If the fears arrive, they do. If they don't, they don't. But the control they have over us, the suffocation they bring to our senses, and the stress they bring to our souls is just not worth it.

Maybe, a more authentic and true way to address the fears that leaves formulas behind, and the one that Solomon is pushing is closer to is something like this:

> Fear not, the things you are afraid of *might* very well happen to you. But, if they do, it's alright. They are nothing to be afraid of.[65]

Which really flips the formula on its head in an essential and critical way. The dangers of living life any other way are everywhere. Which might be why Jesus (and Solomon) are so insistent that we not be afraid. Not from storms, not from demons, not from sickness, not from authorities, and not from things we do not understand.[66]

We start to miss out on the beauties of darkness.

We start to miss out on a God that is found in the fear and a God that is found in the places we are so afraid to go.

We start to miss out on the life to live.

This fog of fear consumes and controls, suffocates and obliterates our hearts, our minds, our bodies and our souls. For nothing.

At some point we have to stop being so afraid.

We have to go *there*. We have to look at those trolls and tell them we are not afraid of them any longer. And suddenly they get real quiet.

But there is, potentially, a more deadly troll to deal with. This one is cunning and hidden and comes masked more like a little friend than an enemy, and so we let it hang around and sit with us, often destroying us just as much as the fear.

These are the dreams. *Those* things we are waiting for that will make everything alright. The ifs that promise to fulfill us.

Sex, power, fame, buildings, horses, slaves, wisdom, armies, cars, hotel rooms, vacations, houses, ski trips, businesses, nonprofits, championships, Oscars, Grammys, bank accounts . . .

Those.

> The Master once told of a neighbor in the countryside who had an obsession with acquiring land. "I wish I had more land," he said one day.

"But why?" asked the Master. "Don't you have enough already?"

"If I had more land, I could raise more cows."

"And what would you do with them?"

"Sell them and make money."

"For what?"

"To buy more land and raise a lot of cows."[67]

These, too, are blinding, never-ending cycles that wrap in and around themselves. The first thousand was good, but I need *another* one. And *another*. A *bigger* car. *More* sex. A *better* house. *Two* Oscars A vacation *there* and with *them*.

Then . . .

Which brings up an whole host of interesting questions. Who tells us these things that will make us happy? Who comes up with these formulas?

Who told us we need to be married to be happy?

Who tells us we can't be happy without money?

Who tells us we can't be successful without a new job, without getting that book published, without getting to the Top 10 on iTunes, without having a child, without the remodel, without, without, without?

Are these sources driven by *our* interests or *their* interests? Who is driving this machine and for what reasons?

It would seem that to each one of these desires is just more fear. Sure they are dressed prettier but to every desire is simply another fear.

What if we never get it? What if it never comes true? What if I spend my whole life working for, trying to achieve, sweating for, giving to . . . and never get the one thing I know will make me happy?

What if I do get it and it doesn't make me happy? What then?

Just more fear. Just more idols. More boats. More false gods. More formulas. More distractions. More preoccupations with the things we don't have. And when we are preoccupied with something we don't have, how can we ever realize what we do have right now?

At some point we have to stop being so afraid.

The first "sermon" Jesus gave is called *The Sermon on the Mount*. It's an absolutely stunning and revolutionary piece of language that would have been as confusing, mysterious, and novel then, as it is now.

> Blessed are the poor in spirit,
> for theirs is the kingdom of heaven.
>
> Blessed are those who mourn,
> for they will be comforted.
>
> Blessed are the meek,
> for they will inherit the earth.
>
> Blessed are those who hunger and thirst for righteousness,
> for they will be filled.
>
> Blessed are the merciful,
> for they will be shown mercy.
>
> Blessed are the pure in heart,
> for they will see God.
>
> Blessed are the peacemakers,
> for they will be called children of God.
>
> Blessed are those who are persecuted because of righteousness,
> for theirs is the kingdom of heaven.[68]

We can read these as formulas. Blessed are those who mourn because when you mourn you are comforted and, therefore, we should all try to mourn.

If I mourn, then I'll be happy.

Or we can read this in a different way, a way that Solomon seems to be leading us; and in a way that leads us to one last troll, which we have to let go of, beyond the fears and the desires dressed up as fears.

We've got to let go of the future completely—which, if you think about it, is the only place where fears and desires ever live anyway. They live in our head with things that *may* or *may not* happen. They live in the same spot as the islands and the boats and the winds and the currents.

They never live *now*.

Maybe what Jesus is trying to illustrate is the truly world-altering idea that *even* when you are mourning, there is *still* life to live. The blessed is here, now, right at this moment . . .

If I just had money.
Let it go. Blessed are you right now.

If I just had a little more confidence.
Let it go. Blessed are you right now.

If my father hadn't died.
Let it go. Blessed are you right now.

If I was only stronger.
Let it go. Blessed are you right now.

If only the world worked better, if only the systems were fixed,
if only that never happened.
Let it go. Blessed are you right now.

If only I didn't have to forgive them again.
If only he would listen this time. If only she would respond.
Let it go. Blessed are you right now.

If only I could have let him know how I really felt and beat the crap out of him.
Let it go. Blessed are you right now.

If only they stopped making fun of me, and stopped being critical, and stopped telling me that I'm too nice or too forgiving or too loving or too moral or too anything.
Let it go. Blessed are you right now.

What are you afraid of?

What are you waiting for?

There is life to live right this very second. Right now.

Enjoy,
appreciate,
soak in,
take in,
be present
with
every
day
of
every
second
with
every
moment
of
life
that
you
have
right
in front of you.

Now that's what living looks like.

At some point we have to stop.

Throw away the formulas. Look the fears in the eyes. Look the desires in the eyes. Look any future prognosis or prediction in the eye and start living.

Let Solomon's words sink in.

> *I know that there is nothing better for people than to be happy and to do good while they live. That each of them may eat and drink, and find satisfaction in all their toil—this is the gift of God.*[69]

> *So I saw that there is nothing better for a person than to enjoy their work, because that is their lot. For who can bring them to see what will happen after them?*[70]

There is nothing better than to be happy and to do good while they live. Eat drink and find satisfaction in everything? Really? There's nothing better?

> *This is what I have observed to be good: that it is appropriate for a person to eat, to drink and to find satisfaction in their toilsome labor under the sun during the few days of life God has given them—for this is their lot. Moreover, when God gives someone wealth and possessions, and the ability to enjoy them, to accept their lot and be happy in their toil—this is a gift of God. They seldom reflect on the days of their life, because God keeps them occupied with gladness of heart.*[71]

Wealth and possessions aren't bad, but they are only good if we are able to enjoy them. And this is their problem. More often than not, they only bring more fear and more desire and less enjoyment and less satisfaction.

Stop being afraid of losing them and stop holding on to the desire to get more. Enjoy them now. *This* is a gift of God.

> *Do not say, "Why were the old days better than these?" For it is not wise to ask such questions.*[72]

You who are young, be happy while you are young, and let your heart give you joy in the days of your youth. Follow the ways of your heart and whatever your eyes see . . . [73]

So then, banish anxiety from your heart and cast off the troubles of your body, for youth and vigor are meaningless.[74]

Anytime we start asking about past thens or future thens, we are not living in the now.

Let the memories and the imaginations go.

A person can do nothing better than to eat and drink and find satisfaction in their own toil. This too, I see, is from the hand of God, for without him, who can eat or find enjoyment?[75]

So I commend the enjoyment of life, because there is nothing better for a person under the sun than to eat and drink and be glad. Then joy will accompany them in their toil all the days of the life God has given them under the sun.[76]

Nothing better? Again. Solomon keeps repeating this mantra over and over again.

Enjoy life. Eat and drink and be glad in every moment.

This is living.

This is what God gives us. Not a better scenario but being able to live in any scenario with life and joy and satisfaction and gladness and contentment.

Blessed is the *now*.

Go, eat your food with gladness, and drink your wine with a joyful heart, for God has already approved what you do. Always be clothed in white, and always anoint your head with oil. Enjoy life with your wife, whom you love, all the days of this meaningless life that God has given you under the sun—all your meaningless days. For this is your lot in life and in your toilsome labor un-

der the sun. Whatever your hand finds to do, do it with all your might, for in the realm of the dead, where you are going, there is neither working nor planning nor knowledge nor wisdom.[77]

Eat your food. Drink your wine. Enjoy life with the one you love in this life of vapor.

With all your might!

The problem, for most of us, is not that we are missing something; the problem is our ability to enjoy what is here with intensity and an immersion of our senses. The problem is not that we are missing something extraordinary; it's that we are so busy running after that extraordinary thing that we have failed to find the life available now in the ordinary.[78]

The problem is not the God who fills the world with color, but the worship of black and white idols who are constantly enticing us to a brighter future that will never exist and, in reality, is far more boring and dull than the bright vibrant one already here, if we would just open our eyes.[79]

Smash the trolls and their idols to pieces. Open your eyes.

At some point, we have to smell the rain. Hear the waves. Taste the salt. Feel the sun. See life, not through the lens of a camera or the photo when you get home, but when you are there present, alive, and awake.[80]

Smell the burnt noodles. Hear the kids screaming. Taste the sweat dripping from your forehead because the air conditioner broke. Feel the greasy floors on your bare feet. See life not through memories of *that* vacation or the anticipation of *that* vacation or the anger that you never get one, but when you are there, present, alive, and awake.

Stop waiting for something and start experiencing everything.

Enjoy,
taste,
smell,
hear,
let your senses come alive,

be happy,
enjoy,
banish anxiety,
cast off troubles,
let your heart give you joy,
eat your food with gladness,
find satisfaction in your toil,
enjoy work,
drink wine with a joyful heart . . .

I commend,
go,
there is nothing better,
I have observed to be good,
I know . . .

Is it possible that *this* is even . . . *eternal* life?

The phrase is thrown around a lot. It has become the biggest and greatest "then" to ever exist. It is the massive carrot for so much of religion. It will start someday and solve all of our problems at some point if all of the "ifs" have been properly checked off.

It's the happy island after we die. But is that how it is supposed to be understood? Doesn't that contradict so much of everything else that has been said?

What if eternal life is not time going on forever (which is arguably not the best translation of those words anyway), which would simply mean that time still rules our lives with its future and pasts. But, instead, eternal life is a way of living in which time fades away into the background because the present is so consuming that we are no longer constrained by time.

We have all experienced this:

It's one in the morning already?
We have to leave?
That was three hours long?
I can't believe it. Where has the time gone?

What if eternal life begins now? Not someday. What if this way of truly living *is* the start of eternal life? What if this is why Jesus speaks so often about this new way of life beginning *now* and not just someday?

Bathe in awe.
Soak in wonder.
Swim in mystery.
Immerse yourself in whoa.

It's here and it's now and it's more than a cheap emotion; it's a way of seeing and perceiving the greatness and grandeur, the microscopic and magnificent, and finding the divine in the ordinary, the ultimate in the average, and the eternal in the present.[81]

This is [eternal] life.

Rob Bell tells the story of The Rabbi of Krakow. It goes something like this:

> The Rabbi of Krakow falls asleep and has a dream. In his dream he sees a treasure under a bridge in a faraway city. So he wakes up, and like most people do with dreams of treasures, he figures it to be true.
>
> He travels for many miles and eventually ends up in the city. After traveling around the city, and searching for many days, he finds the bridge. It's not a large bridge, but it is guarded.
>
> So, the Rabbi sneaks down a river bank at dusk and begins making his way to the bridge. He eventually reaches the dirt and shrubs underneath it and begins to dig.
>
> Fairly quickly, however, a guard hears him and calls out, "You, sir, come here right away."
>
> So, the Rabbi obeys and climbs up the embankment to the bridge. When he gets there, the guard is waiting along with a police officer. The officer looks at the Rabbi and asks him, "What are you doing down there?"

"Well . . ." he sheepishly answers. "You wouldn't believe me. It's strange."

"What is it?"

"Well, I had a dream. And in the dream there was a treasure buried under this bridge. I'm trying to find it."

The officer begins to laugh hysterically. "I would expect more out of a Rabbi," he roars. "You seriously believe in dreams like that?"

"Yes," the Rabbi answers.

"Ha. If I believed in dreams like that, I would be heading to Krakow. I had a dream of a great treasure buried beneath the bed of a Rabbi there."

The Rabbi smiled and said "Thank you" before returning home.

What if we stopped, got rid of our quests for fame, power and fortune, looked our fears in the eyes, along with our desires, along with the futures and pasts and started to see, feel, taste, hear, and smell all of the life and living to be done right

this very second

in

this

ordinary

moment

that

is

happening

as

you

read

these

words?

eleven

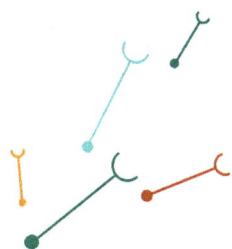

fear god.

The pendulum swings. We see them all the time. The overreaction. The swaying from one extreme to the other, and the struggle to find ourselves in the middle, if there is a middle.

So we are confronted with a pendulum here. At least I was.

We have thrown out God, we have thrown out fear, and we have thrown out desire and left ourselves with very little except eating and drinking with all of our might. Is this when we all quit our job, spend our savings (if we have any), and move to Costa Rica with some friends and sit stoned on a beach all day?

Is that all that's left? Is that how we are to end up living?

> YOLO (You Only Live Once)
> It's time to party!
> Live it up!
> We gotta live like we're dying!
> We only have tonight so let's make it happen, girl!

I like to think that that line of thinking—about being ready to let that pendulum go flying the other direction—is exactly where Solomon wants us. Maybe that's where he ended up for a while. Either way, he throws out this little zinger, almost as a conclusion, that might put a hold on the pendulum racing toward the YOLO train.

> *Much dreaming and many words are meaningless. Therefore fear God.*[82]

Fear God.

Really? As much as I was ready for something, I wasn't quite ready for that one. Is that where we end up, Solomon? If this was Yacine at Starbucks, I might have just walked out.

It stung. I was irritated. I had thought we were supposed to throw fear out the window, and I had thought God was a mystery. Suddenly we were back to the old "fear God" that the preacher on the *Old Time Gospel Hour* would yell at everyone.

What does that even *mean*? *Fear God*?

Which made me stop and start again. What *does* it mean? What seems to fit with all of these seemingly random and incoherent descriptions *and* with life and experience and spirit and breath?

So I started with what it *doesn't* mean, which always seems like a good thing.

Fear Humans

Some will say *fear God*, but what they really mean is to be afraid of the *human* who happens to know how God feels about me, and that human will make sure an appropriate insult is given.

But that's not fearing God.

Fear the Law

Some will say *fear God*, but what they really mean is that I should fear the law because the law says what can and cannot be done. And the law will have its justice—usually at the hands of a person who likes to bring about justice "for the law" and "for God."

But that's not fearing God.

Fear Sermons

Some will say *fear God*, but what they really mean is the pastor (who is speaking for God) now gets a chance to make me feel like crap. If you've never heard one of those sermons, consider yourself lucky. If you have, I'm sorry, but . . .

. . . that's not fearing God.

Fear Yourself

Some will say *fear God*, but what they really mean is that someone (who is speaking for God) will now make me feel as though I am not worth it, not enough, or that I'm missing something in my essential person. This is called shame and . . .

. . . that's not fearing God because shame has no place with God.

Fear Humiliation

Remember when people used to have to put a red "A" on their chest if they were caught in adultery? Remember when homosexuals were told they needed to leave churches because they are gay?

That's still not fearing God.

Fear the New

As that clip from *Toy Story 3* said, people are often under the impression that if it's a new idea of God, it can't be true. Some will say *fear God* and, ironically, they are so afraid of what a new idea of God could look like that they never allow themselves to go there and fear God. Words like "heretic" and "false prophet" are often thrown around by people with a fear of the new.

But that's not fearing God. In fact, it's a fear of fearing God.

Fear Evil

It's interesting how many times people will confuse God and Satan. For example, one of the main words to describe evil, or the devil, throughout the Bible is "accuser"—the one who is bringing up all the wrongs. So . . . who would be holding up the signs and bringing up the sins in the first place? Who is it that is constantly accusing me?

That's not fearing God.

Fear Hell

Fire and brimstone. It seems like many times *fear God* really means *fear hell* becausem, they say, God will send me there, and the same person telling me that God will send me there happens to know who is going there, who isn't, and where I fit in.

It's still not fearing God.

Fear the Consequences

This really sums up what most people have meant by *fear God*. It indicates some kind of consequence that God may, or may not, be carrying out. But even if God is doling out consequences, it's still not about fearing God, it's about fearing what will happen to me.

Typically, humans will carry out these consequences based on the law and in the name of God. And they will come through a sermon with some form of shame and humiliation and speak of heretics and hell—all of which, in my opinion, is actually closer to the devil than God, but usually comes from God's "followers."

Is *that* what Solomon meant after all of this letting go, this mystery, these fears and desires and this idea of living every moment for all that it has? Be scared of how God can hurt me or, even better, just remind everyone else how God can hurt them?

Really? There's no way.

Solomon said to "fear God," not "fear what God will do to me." To put it another way, so I could at least understand it, I asked myself: What if there were no consequences with God?

Then what would it look like to *fear* God?

Next, I decided I would go to the Bible. After all, the Bible is where most of the ideas of this God and this God's followers come from, and where, in fact, "Fear God" even appears . . . so, what does the Bible say?

A lot. But I'm not sure it helped that much.

The first place it's mentioned is in Genesis within the story of Abraham.[83]

God has just destroyed Sodom and Gomorrah because, according to Ezekiel, they lived in luxury, were proud, gluttonous, lazy, ignored the oppressed and poor, put on airs, and lived obscene lies.[84]

So God destroys a city. This would be something to fear, I suppose. Lot, however, is saved by God because he's "righteous." Right after the city is destroyed, and his wife is gone, his two daughters get him drunk and have sex with him in order to have children.

Wait, this is the "good guy" that God saves? Did *he* fear God?

Regardless, Lot's uncle Abraham (God's chosen man) leads his people into the Negev. It's there that he lies to the king of the region and tells him that his wife is actually his sister because "there is surely no fear of God in this place."

So Abraham lies to the king to save himself and Lot (who has two daughters who are pregnant with his kids) because he's worried there's no fear of God in this place?

For the record, the king who leads *this* place acts more kind and humble than anyone else in that section of the story.

Of course, the stories keep going and going and going . . .

Joseph, one of Abraham's descendants, is playing a trick on his brothers (which is a really good trick and a really good story, but it's still a trick), and while he's doing that he says, "Now, I know you fear God . . ."

He does?

A bunch of Egyptians die when the Red Sea crushes them and the Israelites "fear the Lord," which makes sense because God has apparently just destroyed their enemies.

Mary, the mother of Jesus, is told she's going to have a baby and she sings about God's mercy extending to those who fear God.[85] In the same chapter, Zechariah sings a song about the same baby and says how great it is that they will now be able to serve without fear.[86]

So they are not supposed to fear God anymore? Or are they?

Jesus eventually starts speaking himself and he doesn't talk too much about fearing God, at all. He does say in one very confusing passage:

> I tell you, my friends, do not be afraid of those who kill the body and after that can do no more. But I will show you whom you should fear: Fear him who, after your body has been killed, has authority to throw you into hell. Yes, I tell you, fear him. Are not five sparrows sold for two pennies? Yet not one of them is forgotten by God. Indeed, the very hairs of your head are all numbered. Don't be afraid; you are worth more than many sparrows.[87]

It sounds like *if* I was going to be afraid of anything, I should be afraid of the one who can throw me into hell, *but* I shouldn't be afraid of anything.

Then we have this one:

> The chief priests and the teachers of the law heard this and began looking for a way to kill him, for they feared him, because the whole crowd was amazed at his teaching.[88]

The chief priests and teachers of the law were the religious leaders of the day who were often at the blunt end of Jesus' criticisms. They were getting most things wrong. But they did fear him and his new ideas.

And then they killed him. That fear didn't seem to help *them*.

And suddenly these words are being used as a descriptor. In the book of Acts alone we have:

God-fearing women[89]
God-fearing Greeks[90]
God-fearing Gentiles[91]
God-fearing Jews[92]
a God-fearing centurion and his family[93]

And I'm still not exactly sure what it means.

Because Romans says:

> The Spirit you received does not make you slaves, so that you live in fear again . . .[94]

But Second Corinthians says:

> We know what is to fear the Lord.[95]

And Philippians says:

> Work out your salvation with fear and trembling.[96]

But 1 John says:

> God is love. Whoever lives in love lives in God, and God in them . . . There is no fear in love. But perfect love drives out fear, because fear has to do with punishment. The one who fears is not made perfect in love.[97]

And the Bible ends with stuff like this:

> Who will not fear you, Lord, and bring glory to your name?[98]

There are many more verses, including the 365 times that Jesus says "do not be afraid"—none of which do anything to help me figure out what it means to fear God.

But they do help me understand that the Bible is not a dictionary or an instruction manual, nor was it written by God on a laptop in a few days. It is a collection of books, poems, rants, songs, stories, letters, and accounts put all together in cultures and languages very different from ours, and one another. And when we read the Bible, it's confusing and contradictory and not always very easy to understand.

Which is probably part of the point. The Bible was never meant to be the point. It was never meant to be understood in *that* way. It was meant to point to things that we can taste, see, feel, and experience with our own souls.

Which is what life is always about anyway.

The Bible is more like a menu.[99] You can describe Thai tacos all day, but until you taste them for yourself, you'll never know how that spicy peanut sauce, jack and white cheddar cheeses, chicken, cilantro, and red onions on a lightly fried corn tortilla taste.

Many people are consumed with studying a menu and wondering why they are always hungry and thirsty while debating descriptions of things they may have never tasted. Or ordered.

I figured, maybe the point was to find it myself? Use my brain, which God gave me. Use the Spirit (breath) of God, which Jesus said is here and experience what this whole *fear God* is talking about?

So, I started thinking about my two uncles.

One of my uncles was just named "Uncle." He lived in New Jersey, near the beach, and drove a yellow Mustang. When you just go by "Uncle," you've made it in life. He doesn't even need a name, because he's "Uncle" on the shore with his yellow Mustang.

But Uncle had a bearskin rug in his upstairs bedroom. As much as I loved the yellow Mustang when I was a third-grader, I hated the bearskin rug. In fact, I never went into that room if I didn't have to, and I rarely went upstairs if I didn't have to because that rug scared me.

I was afraid of it.

Of course, I knew it wouldn't do anything to me—it was dead. Every time I went in there, it was dead.

But I *was* afraid.

I have another uncle: Uncle Jimmy. Uncle Jimmy was similar to Uncle in that I always looked forward to going to Uncle Jimmy's house. Uncle Jimmy is a master model builder and always had a scene out of World War II in his basement filled with hundreds of models: planes, tanks, fake trees, and little soldiers. I could sit there and stare at them for hours.

Sometimes he would let me play with the airplanes. Heaven.

But Uncle Jimmy was also a hunter. One year, he returned with a bear and a story. The bear almost killed him. He would tell us the story every time we asked. He was behind a tree and this bear was coming at him. He shot it multiple times, unloading his gun, but it kept coming at him. At one point, there was nothing between him and this bear but a tree branch that had temporarily caught the bear while my Uncle Jimmy was trying to reload his gun, and accidentally spilling bullets on the ground.

Finally, the bear turned around and headed for a nearby lake, knowing it was near death. My Uncle Jimmy went after the bear, pulled it out of the lake, and had it stuffed and hung on his office wall (as though it was coming after him, just like it was when it was caught on that tree branch).

I would stare at that thing.

I was afraid of it. Not that it would kill me, but I was afraid of everything else: the story, the danger, the awe of it, really.

The *awe* of it. The *mystery* of it.

There is a Hebrew word that means "great, accomplishment, arise, too high to comprehend, marvelous, miraculous, wondrous," and "wonder-ful." The word is *palah*. The bears were *palah*. Those bears weren't going to *do* anything to me, but they triggered *great* feelings of, *accomplishment* (my uncles'), *marvel*, *wonder* and *mystery* in that elementary brain of mine, when I saw them.

This got me thinking that there are, apparently, some forms of fear that are not about being afraid of what will happen, but rather being over-whelmed by the wonder and awe and mystery of the whole story.

I like that.

There's a story in the Bible about a woman who was barren. I don't know if you've ever known someone who has tried to have a child and can't, or maybe you are that person, but it can be a very humiliating and difficult burden to carry.[100]

A man comes to this barren woman and tells her that she is going to have a child. She's pretty excited, obviously.

The woman goes to her husband and says, "Honey, I've got some good news. A man of God came to me, and his appearance was like the appearance of an angel of God—very awesome." When she says "awesome," she is talking about *palah* awesome. She is talking about *fearful* awesome. About *whoa* awesome.

She keeps talking to her husband and tells him that she didn't ask where the man came from and that the man didn't say his name. But the man said we're going to have a child—a son! And this son is never going to drink wine, grape juice or eat fresh or dried grapes—really anything that has to do with grapes—and he's never going to shave his head, and he's never going to go near a dead person for his entire life.

Strange.

But we're going to have a son!

I don't know what her husband's reaction was, but I imagine he smiled, laughed, and wondered what the deal was with the grapes and hair cutting, and if this was all really going to happen. We do know he went and prayed to God saying, "Please let the man of God whom You have sent come to us again that he may teach us what to do for the boy who is to be born."

So the man of God did come back. The wife was working in a field when he returned. She quickly ran to her husband saying, "He's here! He's back!" Her husband runs to meet the man of God and quickly confirms that he is the one who came before. He then asks the man for more information. "Tell me more! What's his future? What's his job? What's this all look like?"

To which the man says something like, "Chill out. I already told your wife. She knows."

At this point, the husband doesn't know what the deal is with this mystery man. But the story says the husband asks the man if he can cook him up a young goat. The man replies, "Though you keep me here, I won't eat your food. If you're going to prepare a young goat, then offer it to God."

Interesting.

Can I make you dinner?

No. If you're going to make dinner, offer it to God. I'm not staying.

Then the husband asks the man a question. He says, "What is your name, so that when your words come to pass, we may honor you?"

In their culture, the word "name" meant much more than it does to us today. We call our kids whatever we want to call them, because we like the sound of the name. It might have some history in our family or it might represent something meaningful to us. However, in the time of our story, names were more than a label. They represented that person, in every way. Their essence. Who they were. Names were, in a sense, giving identification to their personality, their stances, and their future. There was a lot of weight in a name.

So, when the husband asks the man about his name, we have to imagine there is a lot more going on here. He's asking him to identify his essence. "Who are you? What's your deal? There's something going on here and I need to know, if this all comes true, who am I supposed to thank?"

The man of God replies, "Why do you ask my name, seeing it is wonderful?"

That word is palah. In other words: "Why are you asking what I'm all about when you are experiencing something that is?"

great
accomplishment
arise
too high to comprehend
marvelous
miraculous
wondrous
and wonderful.

"Who do you think I am? What else would I be? Didn't I just tell you some of the best news you've ever heard? What are you trying to figure out?"

Then the husband went with some grain and a young goat and made an offering to God. The story says that when the flame went up toward the sky, the man ascended on the flame up to heaven. And the husband and wife fell on their faces and they knew that the man had been an angel of the Lord.

And they were very afraid and said to themselves "We have seen God!"

They *saw* God?

How can I be grumpy driving to work on an early morning because it's cold and dark and too early and then see the sun rising and my whole attitude changes?

Sunrise, what is your name?

A few weeks ago at our church, we asked people who were hurting to stand up. They had to express incredible courage and vulnerability to do that, but when they did, we asked other people to stand with them. They didn't have to say anything; they just needed to touch them some-how and stand with them. Maybe cry with them. Something happened that morning. It was bigger than emotional manipulation or sadness. It was felt in a deeper place.

"What is your name?"

Have you ever had a conversation that was more than words? Have you ever listened to a song that was more than notes? Have you ever seen a piece of art that was more than colors? Have you ever tasted a piece of bread that was more than flavor?

"What is *your* name?"

"Why do you ask my name, seeing it is wonderful?"

It's interesting that some of those religious leaders who feared Jesus were also indignant at the wonderful things that Jesus was doing.[101] They were angry with wonder. Not only did they miss out on a moment of palah, they missed seeing God.

Yet they were afraid. For all the wrong reasons.

It seems like there are still a lot of people in that spot. They can recite every verse and tell you exactly where it comes from. They can detail every systematic theology there is and debate you on it for hours. They can quote books and theologians and mystics and church fathers and they can tell you how we all need to be more afraid of God.

And yet they never see wonder.

They can pray with the most eloquent words ever used and sing the most beautiful melodies ever heard and answer the most difficult questions ever asked.

And yet they are aren't very good at seeing God when God hits their eyes, ears, noses, and hands.[102]

They don't fear God. In *that* way.

Which brings us back to what it means to *live*. It would seem that fearing God means to see God in every moment with the same wonder and awe and majesty as when I saw those bearskins and when that couple learned they were going to have a baby.

It's sad that *that* has been turned into something to make us afraid. I hate to think what kinds of things we miss out on and what kinds of moments we don't live when we're so busy being afraid of consequences from God, instead of God.

If we're ever talking about a fear that brings shame, boredom, depression, anger, violence, hate, jealousy, pride, other fears, or is an excuse to shame others, or make them afraid, then it's not *fear God* the way it should be.

There is a fear that makes me not want to live and there is a fear that makes me want to live more than I ever have. *That's* the fear we're talking about.

Our *fearing God* is all about truly living.

Soak it in for what it is. Be moved by it. Acknowledge the proper place it comes from. *Fear God*.

If your definition of fearing God doesn't bring life, than I don't think it's the right definition.

I don't know if you've ever been to a chiropractor or simply had someone pop your back, but when you do, there's something that feels so good about it. It's as though things are balanced again. The pendulum has stopped swinging from side to side and there is a centering that happens even within your own body.

The more I read what Solomon said, the more I thought that's was this fear is supposed to do. It should align us. It should align me.

> *I have seen the burden God has laid on the human race.*
>
> *He has made everything beautiful in its time.*
>
> *He has also set eternity in the human heart; yet no one can fathom what God has done from beginning to end.*
>
> *I know that there is nothing better for people than to be happy and to do good while they live. That each of them may eat and drink, and find satisfaction in all their toil—this is the gift of God. I know that everything God does will endure forever; nothing can be added to it and nothing taken from it. God does it so that people will fear him.*[103]

At first glance, it didn't make a lot of sense to me. What is the *it* that God does? What are the *its* that God does so that people will fear God?

> God makes everything beautiful. So that people will fear God?
>
> God puts eternity in the human heart. So that people will fear God?
>
> God has made it so no one can fathom what God does. So that people will fear God?
>
> God has given everyone a gift of being able to enjoy eating, drinking, and finding satisfaction. So that people will fear God?

None of these are consequence-driven. They are *palah-*, *whoa-*, and *awe*-driven. Each of them instills a fear, not of being hurt, but that I might be missing something because my perspective, or my alignment, is off.

There is something about looking up at the stars, thinking about galaxies and rays of light cruising at 186,000 miles a second that take 2.5 millions of years to get to us that just aligns things.[104]

There is more. These kinds of things have been said many times before including Rob Bell's masterful version of them in *Everything is Spiritual* and his most recent book *What We Talk About When We Talk About God*, but it's hard to hear them too often. Let them impact you—whether it's your first time or you've heard them before.

Let your back crack.

> The observable universe is the region of space that is visible to us from Earth. The entire universe is estimated to be 93 billion light years across, even though most would say that the universe is only 13.8 billion light years old. So that means we can't see anything beyond 13.8 billion light years but because the universe is expanding, and has been expanding for those 13.8 billion light years and we can calculate that rate of expansion, we estimate 93 billion light years across.[105]

Our sun is one of 400 billion stars in our galaxy.

There are a hundred billion galaxies out there with a potential number of stars in the 10^{22}. That's the number one followed by 22 zeroes.[106]

Beyond that, most would say that the entire universe—beyond that which is observable—is possibly infinite or at least without a border.

In other words, it's very, very, very large. Beyond-understanding kind of large.

But more than that, it's expanding. And even more than that, it's expanding at an accelerating speed (which no one believed until recently), which means that one day in the future, humans will theoretically look up into space and see . . . nothing.

Physicist Brian Greene elaborates on this saying that because the expansion is so fast, eventually the speed of light will not be able to overcome the distance.

> So astronomers in the far future, looking out into deep space, will see nothing but an endless stretch of static, inky, black stillness. And they will conclude that the universe is static and unchanging and populated by a single central oasis of matter that they inhabit—a picture of the cosmos that we definitively know to be wrong. Now, maybe those future astronomers will have records handed down from an earlier era, like ours, attesting to an expanding cosmos teeming with galaxies, but would those future astronomers believe such ancient knowledge? Or would they believe in the black, static empty universe that their own state-of-the-art observations reveal? I suspect the latter.[107]

Talk about *whoa*. We can predict that in a far, distant future, scientists will discern the wrong information from everything that the facts point out to them. What does *that* mean?

Is *that* possible today?

Some scientists don't stop there. They say that not only is the universe expanding and not only is it speeding up, but there might be other universes and that we're part of a multiverse, or multiple universes. How many?

Some say there might be infinite universes. Infinite universes with the size of our own? *That* big? Infinite? Of course, this brings up some wild ideas relating to quantum physics and what the present way we perceive reality even means, including things like: "What is reality?" and "What is free-will?" and "How does God play into all of this?"

At some point my head starts to hurt and I just stop. But these ideas are apparently playing with lots of people's heads, leading some scientists and philosophers to say things like, "Fundamental physics is in a metaphysical mess and needs help."[108]

When they say it needs help, they are saying it needs help from areas *other* than science. We've never known more . . . only to find out how little we do know, or in some cases, even *can* know.

Why do you ask my name?

And we go from that kind of largeness to a single human hair, and the fact that one million atoms can line up side by side on that hair. A single grain of sand contains 22 quintillion atoms (that's 18 zeroes, if you were wondering). But beyond that, there are 150 subatomic particles (which are all smaller than those atoms) that have been discovered.

In other words, there are very, very small things in this very, very large universe.

All of which is pretty hard to comprehend. There are multiple YouTube videos that do a great job, but at the end of the day, we still can't really grasp it.

It's just *too* big. And *too* small. It's, in a sense, *too* marvelous to comprehend. And yet, it all combines to create such stunning and beautiful and palah moments every day . . .

Green fields with rays of yellow sun shining on them, as though they are glowing.

An Amazon Rainforest so thick with trees that no light gets through and interspersed with rivers and streams and more than one-third of all the species on our planet.

Creatures like dolphins, whales, sea urchins, and great white sharks.

Clouds, rain, and images that look like they belong in fantasy or science fiction movies—with lightning and fireballs surrounding a lava-spewing volcano.

The Bubble Nebula[109]. Images of this nebula look almost like a bubble—the same kind you would find floating through the air at a kid's party. But this nebula is 11,000 light years away, which means that the Bubble Nebula we see today is the one that existed when Earth was entering the Neolithic period and consisted of no more than 5 million people. The Bubble Nebula is almost 60 trillion miles across and has surrounding stars that are 45 times more massive than our own sun.

Perspective and alignment: It's a beautiful thing because once we start to really get it, it's hard not to think there just might be something bigger than me, and if there's something bigger than me, well, sitting on the beach in Costa Rica may not be all that life has to offer.

This is probably why most societies throughout history have always worshiped something bigger than themselves, whether it's a volcano, thunder, the stars, the moon, the sun, a god, a spirit, or something else.[110] We feel small in the face of such majesty and magic and wonder.

And if you think about it, it's when we feel *that kind of small* that we start to do things *bigger* than ourselves. Unfortunately, we may be the first society in a while where having something bigger than ourselves isn't important. We find *ourselves* plenty enthralling, which is where Solomon would probably remind us to *fear God*.

And start living.

David Foster Wallace, in his astounding and brilliant commencement speech from 2008, uses words like *automatic, unconscious, boring, frustrating,* and *crowded* to talk about "living in a spot where I am the center of the world." He talks about *meaningful, sacred, on fire with the same force that lit the stars, compassion,* and *love* to talk about a place where we pay attention to what is around us.[111]

We start to pay attention to the awe around us and the people around us. The people who desire connection and who need the gifts that we can give.

Is it possible that this "fear of God" might not only describe what it's like to live life fully each moment, but that it might actually inspire us to live it better for ourselves and to bring that life to others?

> *Do not be overrighteous, neither be overwise—why destroy yourself?*
>
> *Do not be overwicked, and do not be a fool—why die before your time?*
>
> *It is good to grasp the one and not let go of the other.*

Whoever fears God will avoid all extremes.[112]

I've heard plenty of messages about being too wicked and the consequences that lie within. I'm not sure I've ever heard anyone warn me about being too righteous or too wise and destroying myself in the process?

The pendulum can swing both ways.

Palah, wonder, awe. It's good to sit in the middle—to keep a hold of both and not let go. Whoever fears God will avoid all extremes. What a great line.

It's the rigid over-righteous who definitely need their back cracked with some wonder.

But . . .

It's the rigid over-wicked who definitely need their back cracked with a reminder that wonder is something way bigger than us and we probably don't need to ask what its name is.

And when things are in alignment, it's just as hard telling people they are going to hell as it is getting trashed and finding a girl at the bar as it is to ignore people who have need for connection and generosity and love.

There's just too much life out there.

There's just too much living to do to get stuck in extremes.

There's just too much *wonder, awe, mystery*, and good *palah* to become consumed with anything less.

We must create. We must expand. We must give.

We must love.

twelve

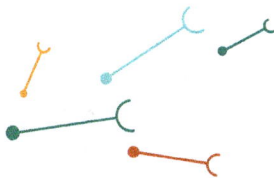

love.

But.

It's one of those very small, but incredibly powerful words. Powerful enough to shatter and smash other words, with which it's associated, into oblivion.

Honey, I really do love you. I think we're great together, *but* . . .

Kids, I know you all want to go get ice cream tonight, *but* . . .

I'm not a racist, *but* . . .

We really love the church, and it's been great for our family, *but* . . .

Perhaps even worse than erasing the words that come before it, *but* transforms the other words into something manipulative or patronizing or coercive. "Butter them up," we say. (Which just happens to begin with "but.")

There is a section of the Bible, so often read at weddings, that it has become "the wedding passage." That is really too bad. Only reading these words at weddings is like only putting that bottle of fine, aged bourbon in a glass of Coke. Sure, it works, but it's so much better and valuable than *that*.

The section of words I'm talking about is 1 Corinthians 13. Chances are good that you've heard it somewhere, maybe a wedding. "Love is patient, love is kind . . ." It might be one of the most powerful, most moving, most inspiring, and strong passages in all of the Bible, and to make it synonymous with a new bride and groom figuring out how to squeeze their toothpaste just waters it down too much.

All of this brings us to the words *love* and *but*. When you ask people about *love*, you will often hear the word *but* not too far behind, especially with certain religious language.

Love . . . *but* . . . God's wrath and anger are real, too.

Love . . . *but* . . . I don't want to condone or approve of that.

Love . . . *but* . . . It's not *that* easy.

Love . . . *but* . . . Justice. Consequences. Judgment.

Love . . . *but* . . . They are gay; they are Muslims; they are enemies; they are a danger; they are (fill in the blank).

Love . . . *but* . . . That fire will burn forever.

This means that not only is the "love" part erased, but it comes off as a platitude that never had a lot of meat behind it in the first place. Which means that religious people start to become "buts."

Buts defined by dot, dot, dot . . .

Angry, wrathful, non-approving, difficult, judgmental, anti, dot, dot, dot . . . which, according to much of the research (you can start with the book *UnChristian*), is exactly what Christians are known for:

Being buts.

If there is anything we have to learn after letting God roam free, after letting our fears and desires and futures go, and beginning to live each moment while remembering this palah experience of God—and our need to give a gift—it's that love is a requirement.

No buts. Just love. Love period.

It's easy to say the Bible is complicated and confusing on some topics. It is. But not when it comes to love. When asked, Jesus answered that the most important commandment, the most important thing we can do, is to love God and to love others. Jesus goes on to say that all of the other laws hang on these two, just like a door hangs on a hinge.[113]

So loving is the greatest, most important thing I can do and everything else hangs on that. No buts.

Jesus later gives his disciples a new command to love one another. He says that this is how people will know they follow Jesus—by loving one another. So, if the world wants to know if someone follows Jesus, they can look at how well they love other people.[114]

No buts.

Paul then says that love binds compassion, kindness, humility, gentleness, and patience along with bearing with and forgiving others. Love binds them all together in a beautiful, perfect, way. No buts.[115]

In Romans, Paul says that love never harms a neighbor.[116] In other passages, Jesus says that our neighbors are our worst enemies.[117] Paul also says that love is the fulfillment of the law.[118]

In other words, all those rules, all those lists . . . love fulfills them all in doing no harm to *anyone*, ever. No buts.

Jesus says everyone has heard that we are to love our neighbor and hate our enemy, but Jesus comes with a new command: Love your enemies and pray for those who persecute.[119] We can assume that Jesus means to pray for blessings and good crops and good lives for them, not for God to punish them.

Jesus goes on to say that God sends rain and sun to the evil and the good, which sounds a lot like Solomon. Jesus seems to be saying that the rain and sun that grow crops come from God and God sends good things to the good and evil.[120]

No formulas. No buts.

So, *be* like that. Send good things to the good and evil—even your enemies. Then Jesus really ups the ante on this whole love thing and says that everyone loves people who *love* them. In fact, your worst enemies love people who love them; that's why we are supposed to love people who don't love us, just like God does.[121]

No buts.

Paul talks about fruits of the spirit that are love,[122] and the mysterious writer of Hebrews says that we should never give up getting together in order to inspire one another to love.[123]

No buts.

What if churches saw their main point in existence as inspiring, motivating, and challenging one another with new, creative, innovative, and revolutionary ways to love? That would be pretty crazy.

No buts.

Then we really get to some of the more powerful words that people, who like to quote scripture and write it on signs, don't quote or write on signs very often.

> God is love. Whoever lives in love lives in God, and God in them . . . Whoever claims to love God yet hates a brother or sister is a liar. For whoever does not love their brother and sister, whom they have seen, cannot love God, whom they have not seen. And he has given us this command: Anyone who loves God must also love their brother and sister.[124]

Verses like this are pretty blunt and to the point without a lot of buts or dots. If you don't love people, you don't love God. Period. You can claim that you do, but you're a liar. If you love God, you must love your brother and sister—meaning your fellow human beings.

And then there's this one verse which puts a finer point on the whole love thing:

> Dear friends, let us love one another, for love comes from God. Everyone who loves has been born of God and knows God. Whoever does not love does not know God, because God is love.[125]

Everyone who loves has been born of God and knows God? That's in the Bible?

What about people who say certain prayers, follow certain beliefs, hold up signs with quoted scripture, go to religious services of some kind, read the Bible, don't do drugs, and do good things?

What about them?

If those people don't love, they don't know God.
If those people do love, they do know God.

Period.

What about a Muslim who loves? Or a prostitute, or a rapist, or a Buddhist, or an atheist or a terrorist, or someone who has had an abortion? What if they love people?

What if a "Christian" doesn't love?

Well, that's all fine and good, but . . .

We've talked a lot about the mystery and the unknown of God. But if there is one thing we *do* know about God, it is that God is love. The Bible makes this very clear in a variety of ways. And if God is love, than that goes back to some of those critical questions . . . like, if God is all powerful and all loving, then why do bad things happen?

What does it mean to be all-powerful?
What does it mean to be all-loving?
Can something be all-loving and all-powerful at the same time?
What role does freedom play?
Can there be love without freedom?
Can there be complete power and freedom?

What if it's not possible to be all-powerful and all-loving because love and power don't work that way? Does this mean that a God who is absolutely powerful cannot be absolutely loving or that a God who is absolutely loving cannot be absolutely powerful because love never equates with power and power never equates with love?

This might mean that God is not all-powerful—not in the sense that we understand power. We always equate power with control, and control is just *not* love. And if God is love, then God does not control. And if God does not control, well . . .

Certain things will happen because God does not seek to control them. And we are told not to either.

Maybe the power of love, besides being a great idea for song lyrics, is actually the most powerful force in the universe. Maybe our views of power and control are skewed and rarely under the umbrella of love.

We can pull out verses all day long about judging, condoning, retribution, revenge, justice, and hell, but it's hard to ignore a major theme in all of this: love.

Period.

No commas, no buts, no dots, no "what about this?" or "what about that?" or ifs or thens, but just periods.

No excuses.

This brings us to some really important questions like: What is love? What does love look like? What does it mean to love? Can I still love someone and tell them they are an idiot? If I love someone shouldn't I tell them the truth and the consequences?

What *is* love? (As so many songs have asked.)

This is why that wedding passage is so important and critical and huge. It describes love. And if you read the entire letter that it's contained in, you can almost see Paul, the author, pacing back and forth as he says the words about love out loud. (I like to imagine him speaking while someone else transcribes, but who knows . . .)

Either way, Paul is building up to the wedding passage throughout the entire letter, eventually getting to these critical components and descriptors of love. And these are not descriptors of people who love. These are not what we really struggle to show.

Whether we like it or not, these are love.

If what we call love isn't these things, is it love? According to this heavy-duty letter, the answer is no. It might be close, but it's not love.

Love is patient.[126]

There is a great saying along these lines: Anger is an excellent motivator in the short term, but not in the long term. Love is a great motivator in the long term, but not in the short term.

In other words: if you want quick results, use anger. If you want results that will last, use love.

What does this mean for revivals, where lots of people come forward to dedicate their lives to Jesus because they are scared of going to hell?

What does this mean for people who hold up bullhorns and announce that God is going to punish other people?

Which way do we think God would work: short-term results that eventually depart or patient, long-term results that stick?

What does the power of that kind of God look like?

There is a great fable written by Aesop. Read it with some patience.

> THE NORTH WIND and the Sun disputed as to which was the most powerful, and agreed that he should be declared the victor who could first strip a wayfaring man of his clothes. The North Wind first tried his power and blew with all his might, but the keener his blasts, the closer the Traveler wrapped his cloak around him, until at last, resigning all hope of victory, the Wind called upon the Sun to see what he could do. The Sun suddenly shone out with all his warmth. The Traveler no sooner felt his ge-

nial rays than he took off one garment after another, and at last, fairly overcome with heat, undressed and bathed in a stream that lay in his path.

Persuasion is better than Force.[127]

If we're trying to change someone by yelling at them, and forcing them to do something for us *right* now, *right* this second . . . chances are we're not loving them.

Love is kind.

Sometimes kind is a better word than love because with love, we can get away with things that we can't with other words, like kind.

I do love them, but sometimes that means I need to be blunt and call it like it is.

I do love them, but sometimes the best way to love someone is to tell them that they are wrong.

Is it kind to be blunt and call it like it is? Is it kind to tell someone that they are wrong?

Even when I'm upset and even when that person doesn't know anything, and I know everything, I'm supposed to be kind because that's what love is.

Period.

Love does not envy.

Envy is not a word we use too often anymore, though we are saturated with the idea of it in our culture today. Capitalism is practically based on never having enough - on always wanting more. Or better. Or newer. Whether we need them or not. We see them on someone or with someone and we want them too. That's envy.

We're in a culture obsessed with it.

Love doesn't care. Love doesn't want things that other people have; love just wants people to have things that bring them life, whether they deserve it or not.

Love is concerned with the moment and being content in that moment, not waiting for the moment when I get something that I want but don't really need even though I think I do.

They haven't earned that, they don't deserve that, and that's not fair that they got that and I didn't, don't exist in love's world.

Love does not boast.

I don't want to brag, but . . . let me tell you what I did . . .

last night.
yesterday.
for the old lady who lives next door.
at work.
for my husband.
at church.
at the game.
for my kids.
last weekend.

Love is not proud.

Love is humble. Love doesn't think too much of itself or maybe to paraphrase what C. S. Lewis wrote: Love doesn't think less of one's self, it just doesn't think of one's self at all.[128] Which brings up a good question: How do we lose ourself?

We certainly don't try. It's hard to remember the last time I lost something by trying to lose it.

We certainly don't cause it pain. It's hard to remember the last time I lost something by making it hurt. That would seem to only make me more aware of it.

So maybe the answer to being humble is not to go around saying I just want to be humble. Maybe it's about being so present in the moment that we don't even realize we're there. Just like Solomon said.

Love does not dishonor others.

If we are not dishonoring others, we are probably honoring them, which—just like the word kind—is a lot harder to fake.

If I'm going to tell you something, I'm going to honor you with my words.

If I'm going to do something to you, I'm going to honor you with my actions.

If I'm going to tell you something about *them*, I'm going to honor *them* to you with my words and actions.

Even if you, or they, are my enemy.

Period.

Love is not easily angered or provoked or ticked off or irked.

This doesn't mean love is *never* angered or provoked, but it certainly isn't *easily* angered.

Love keeps no record of wrongs.

This one has been translated all kinds of different ways for good reasons. We generally don't like anything close to it. It's often translated that love does not take into account a wrong suffered. One translation has nothing. Another says that one does not rejoice in iniquity.

The Greek words of the Biblical text are . . .

> negative (keep a mental record of events) harm, wrong, mistreatment of someone or something.

My own translation is: Love does not keep track of things that have hurt me so that I can hurt someone later. Love does not remember this one for later—when it will sting the most.

Love doesn't keep a tally of what that person has done to you or to others. Love doesn't treat that person differently because they said something last week that wasn't quite right and now it's really weird and, well, now . . . they need to pay for it.

(Just to be clear, this does not mean things like: he raped me, and I will go on a date with him again. This does not mean: he physically abused me as a child, and now I will go hang out with him for a nice breakfast. Love may not mean remembering in order to harm someone, but it does mean remembering in order to not let someone harm you again.)

Love does not delight in evil but rejoices with the truth.

At first glance this one is a little confusing. What do "not delighting in evil" and "rejoicing with truth" have to do with each other? But the more you think about it, the more they might actually have some connections.

Love doesn't delight in anger, in hypocrisy, in judgment, in power, in greed, or in cheap T-shirts that are made by slave labor, but it does rejoice with grace, mercy, forgiveness, peace, and joy for all people all planet Earth.

Love always protects, always trusts, always hopes, and always perseveres.

Always is a pretty big word that is a lot like a period. No buts, no ifs, no wells, no unlesses; it just always . . .

> protects reputations and feelings.

> trusts someone's motivations.

> hopes that people and their lives will be redeemed and beautiful—as beautiful as our own.

> perseveres until *that* happens.

Love never fails.

If you want something that you can bet 100 percent on, it's love. The letter doesn't say that people who love never fail or that people never fail or that people in the church never fail. It just says that love never fails, which is a pretty powerful thing. In fact, I can't think of anything else on Earth that never fails.

Maybe love is the most powerful thing?

(Just for fun, reread this list and substitute "God" for "love." If God is love, then that means all of these words would apply to God as well. This would also mean that God never fails. Which brings up a whole host of other very interesting questions.)

When love is working, it works. Period.

It's interesting that Paul, who wrote this amazing letter, was once a Pharisee. He was a religious leader of his day. He was a man that persecuted others, judged everyone who wasn't in his camp, and had it all figured out. He knew everything because he had been properly schooled, grew up in the right kind of family, and knew God.

Except, one day, he realized he didn't.

You can almost see him pacing around, reciting these descriptors of love, and then finally stopping. Instead, he begins reviewing his own life, his own transformations, and the things that got to him.

The things that worked in the long term.

Paul slows down and the guy transcribing this letter looks up, wondering if there will be more. Love never fails. Never. It just doesn't. It works every time.

It's what changed me, I can imagine Paul thinking.

Andre Agassi started a school for kids that wouldn't normally get a chance to go to school. Everything started to change in his life, and he wrote this:

> This is why we're here. To fight through the pain and, when possible, to relieve the pain of others. So simple. So hard to see.[129]

We are here to love. Period. It never fails.

> The really important kind of freedom involves attention, and awareness, and discipline, and effort, and being able truly to care about other people and to sacrifice for them, over and over, in a myriad of petty, little, unsexy ways, every day. That is real freedom. The alternative is unconsciousness, the default setting, the "rat race"—the constant gnawing sense of having had and lost some infinite thing.[130]

Remember those caribou running around all over the place? In the rat race of unconsciousness? Love, in that sense, brings freedom from the default, mundane lives we often live and awakes us to the present by giving gifts of love and care to others.

> The truth that is hinted at here is the idea that love is what brings meaning. The one who loves life and embraces others finds meaning in even the most mundane of activities. Food is no longer about sustaining the body but of communing with others, drinking does not simply satisfy a thirst but joins people in celebration, work is not about achieving some future happiness but about filling one's present with worthwhile activity.[131]

Eat your food. Drink your wine. Work with your full effort, because these are the ways we begin to live, to love, and to work alongside a God of wonder and mystery and creation.

It's the love that brings meaning to the vapors. It's the love that enables us to get through the pain, to fight the pain in others, to find life, to enjoy the mystery and the moment, and to fear God.

Love period.

The great Henri Nouwen wrote the following:

> My own desire to be useful, to do something significant, or to be part of some impressive project is so strong that soon my time is taken up by meetings, conferences, study groups, and workshops that prevent me from walking the streets. It is difficult not to have plans, not to organize people around an urgent cause,

and not to feel that you are working directly for social progress. But I wonder more and more if the first thing shouldn't be to know people by name, to eat and drink with them, to listen to their stories and tell your own, and to let them know with words, handshakes, and hugs that you do not simply like them, but truly love them.[132]

The extraordinary in the ordinary. God in the mundane. It's all right there.

But Paul goes on just to make sure we are *really* getting this stuff. He talks about prophecies, which are a pretty big deal for most people who would say they follow a God. Paul writes they will eventually cease. He talks about tongues, the ability to speak the words of God—again, a pretty big deal—and says they will be stilled. He talks about knowledge and how it will pass away.

Paul says that we know in part, we prophesy in part, and when completeness comes, what is in part disappears. In other words, prophecies and tongues and knowledge and answers aren't really the things we're looking for.

And then Paul talks about being a child and growing up. He says when we're children, we act like children, but that stops when we grow up. He talks about seeing reflections and looking in mirrors. He says there will come a time when love is all that remains, when we are truly seen, truly known, and truly visible. When the fog is lifted and all that is left is love.

Maybe the biggest question of all is this: *If* that time is coming, do we even want it?

Do we want it enough to make it happen?

Do we want a time when we no longer point fingers and tell people they are wrong and we are right? Do we want a time when we no longer think of ourselves as better than others? Do we want a time when we no longer get the hit of endorphins from calling someone out and making them small so that we feel bigger? Do we want a time when we no longer feel like we have earned it through our hard work and dedication and they have not?

Do we *even* want that?

If we're honest—if I'm honest—I often love the buts and the dots, not those periods.

The Mission was released in 1986. I was 12 at the time and living in Seattle. I remember my parents took me to the movie and I was pretty bored. The beginning was exciting because a guy was attached to a wooden cross and sent over a waterfall, but other than that, it wasn't my kind of movie.

I watched it 10 years later and was blown away.

The movie follows the story of a Spanish Jesuit missionary named Father Gabriel who visits a South American tribe in an effort to convert them. The story also follows a man named Mendoza, a Spanish slave trader who kills his brother in a fit of rage.

Father Gabriel meets Mendoza who is distraught and on the verge of suicide after killing his brother. Mendoza eventually converts and wishes to become a priest.

There is an amazing scene where Mendoza and Father Gabriel are traveling to meet the tribe. The tribe is located at the top of a large waterfall (the same waterfall that the man went down at the beginning of the movie) and Mendoza insists on carrying all of this old slave gear up the waterfall as a penance for his crime.

The metal helmets, swords, and shields are a burden and Mendoza, try as he might, falls multiple times. Over and over, he tries to get through the mud and up the slippery rocks with the weight behind him, but he can't. Eventually, Father Gabriel grabs a sword and rushes toward Mendoza, cutting the ropes that attach him to the gear he is carrying—and to his past.

Father Gabriel cuts the rope and the dirty, metal swords and helmets go falling down the rocks until they land in the water in a splash of mud and dirt. Mendoza begins weeping uncontrollably and Father Gabriel embraces him.

Love is like *that*. It's using swords, not to slash throats but to cut the ropes that weigh people down. Love removes the burdens, the shame—sometimes the religion—whatever it is that is pulling people down and dragging them backward. Love frees them, liberating them to move forward into something better.

Love breathes life.

So carry a sword with you always—not to harm, but to cut away baggage and pasts and weights.

Paul starts off this section of the letter with the following paragraph that I think actually works better at the end.

> If I speak in the tongues of men or of angels, but do not have love, I am only a resounding gong or a clanging cymbal. If I have the gift of prophecy and can fathom all mysteries and all knowledge, and if I have a faith that can move mountains, but do not have love, I am nothing. If I give all I possess to the poor and give over my body to hardship that I may boast, but do not have love, I gain nothing.[133]

"Nothing" is a big word.

There are many people who would say it's a pretty big deal to speak in the tongues of angels; an equal number of people who would say the same about prophecy. How many would say that someone who can fathom all mysteries and knowledge is someone worth looking up to? Or what about a faith that can move mountains or a person that gives everything they have to the poor or someone who gives their body over to hardship for the sake of someone else?

All pretty big deals.

All nothings without love.

Nothing? Nothing.

Maybe it's time we stop trying to *know* more, stop trying to *know* the God who can't be known, and start loving in order see and experience the God who is love.[134]

Period.

No commas, no ifs, no buts, no dots, just love. Period.

Or there is nothing.

Of course, none of this is easy. There's a reason we don't do it. It's hard. It takes effort and sometimes pain.

Which makes us ask: Can any human really do this? Any of it?

Can *we* even love? And how?

We're just humans. Right?

thirteen

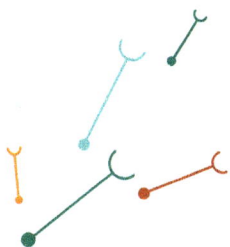

just be human.

Some of my favorite stories about Jesus are near the end of the book of John. They are some of my favorites for the same reasons as Ecclesiastes: they make sense in a deeper way than platitudes and clichés, and they are not the stuff that people usually say in terms of Christianity or religion.

And they are inspiring. Maybe none more than this one.[135]

Jesus is about to die. He knows it. Things aren't looking good. He's been hanging out with a lot of people, but 12 guys have been right there with him, through the good and the bad, the hard and the fun, the fear and the dreams. They have followed him everywhere.

He gives these 12 guys a little speech right before he's taken away by the religious leaders. He says a few really cool things.

First, he says, there is no reason to worry. Jesus says he may be leaving, but that the 12 know where he's going and that he's going to prepare a place for them.

Some take this as Jesus saying he's going to heaven to prepare them (and us) some mansions, but if you put it in the context of his day, Jesus is saying what every groom said to every bride. Couples would be engaged and then the groom would leave to go to his father's house to prepare a room for him and his new bride. When he was ready, he would surprise his bride-to-be, often in the middle of the night, and bring her home.

So maybe Jesus was saying that he's going to heaven to prepare golden mansions or maybe he was saying that he loves them and he's only leaving for the same reasons a groom leaves—not because he doesn't love them, but because he does love them and wants to make things better for them.

The disciples respond, like they often do (which is why they are so great): "Uh, Jesus, actually we *don't* know where you are going. So how are we supposed to know the way?" In other words, "What are we supposed to do?"

Jesus responds with the oft-quoted line: "I am the way. I am the truth. I am the life." Many have interpreted this to mean that Jesus was saying if you want to get to heaven, then you must be a Christian.

I don't see that here.

Jesus goes on to make some statements like, "If you have seen me, you have seen God" and "If you know me, you know God" and "No one comes to God except through me" which imply that Jesus is saying something more along the lines of . . .

I am the best representation of God. If you have an image of God that doesn't match up to me, well, it's probably some kind of idol or boat or formula or god that isn't the God of love, the God of truth, and the God of life. If you want to find *that* God, and *that* life, the way I've been living the things I've been saying *that's* where it's at.

Jesus says he is the *life* that we've been talking about.

This is incredibly important. There are many people who would say they agree with Jesus and the way he lived, *but* . . . that's not how God is. Jesus seems to say the complete opposite here.

None of this, though, to me, is the really amazing thing. After all of this, and assuming his guys are still a little confused, Jesus looks them in the eye and says:

> "Whoever believes in me will do everything I've been doing *and* even greater things."

Everything?

We will do everything that Jesus has been doing? We can live that way, that truth, and that life? That's astounding enough. But Jesus adds more.

You will do *greater* things?

Jesus has turned water into wine. These guys were with him.

He has cleared out the temple and challenged the religious elite. They were there.

He has talked with a Samaritan woman (who he was not supposed to talk to) in a creative, revolutionary way and they saw it.

He has healed an official's son, a paralytic, and a man born blind; he's walked on water, raised someone from the dead, and a lot more. These guys watched him, and were scared out of their minds at what was happening most of the time. And then he has the gall to look them in the eye and say, "You'll do even greater things than me."

What? Is this for real?

So much in Christian language points to God doing everything while we sit around and sing songs on Sunday morning and pray for God to do everything. That's just *not* what Jesus says. He empowers humanity and says *you* are going to change the world. You. Yeah, you.

Me? Yes. *You.*

The Bible is not just a book about humanity's faith in God but God's faith in humanity.[136] And never more so than right here. The Bible is not just a story of humans trying to be gods but of a God becoming a human and saying . . . now *you* live this way, this truth and this life.

This whole story is pretty fantastic. "Don't worry, guys. This is for real. I'm not leaving you to abandon you; I'm leaving like a groom leaves his bride. I'm preparing a place. You know where I'm going."

"Actually, we don't. So how are we going to get there?"

"I'm the way. The way I live, the things I say . . . believe in that stuff and *do* it, and you'll do greater things than me and you'll have life.

"You will rock this planet."

This isn't about waiting for heaven. This isn't about waiting to get to Happy Island someday. This is about pain, life, mystery, fear, love, and the faith of God in us to do it right.

Now.

To live.

That's good stuff. I would imagine that to the 12 disciples it was even good news because it contradicted everything else that was being said at the time. In that sense, it's *still* really good news.

This is *not* Jesus saying you'll be rich and famous. Jesus wasn't rich or famous (at least not in the way we think of famous).

This is *not* about Jesus saying you'll be me. There is always an order to the universe: God, us, them, nature—which means that we are supposed to know our place and our perspective and that there is something bigger.

But this *is* about something the hip-hop artist Common once said: "They hear your soul if you're using it."[137]

The problem with a lot of people is that they aren't using their soul because they don't trust that their soul is worth using. So they silence their soul and wait for some future day, in some happy place, when their soul is worth using again. But that's not what Jesus preaches. Jesus says that your soul is worth using and you should start believing it and start letting people hear the enchanting melody inside of it.

Jesus frequently goes to people who think they are ruined, not enough, not valued, not respected (mostly by religious leaders) and tells them they are beautiful, precious, valued, and worth it. He tells people, who the world has told to go away, that the world actually needs them to be loud and creative and to bring love and passion and let their soul be loud.

Too often we're consumed with becoming some kind of future spiritual superhero and not fully embracing all that we are supposed to be right now, as humans. The stories of Jesus reveal that we are already spiritual and sacred and wonderful; we just need to know it. There is no waiting to get somewhere or to become something; there is realizing what we already are, right now, from our body to our mind to our soul and that God is there. It seems like all the things we are looking for, are already here.[138]

Can you imagine what those disciples must have thought? "Seriously? Us? Greater things? Are you sure? Have you been drinking, Jesus?

"We're not going to be able to do this. Not us. We can barely handle the pain. And this thing of being present, and the mystery, and the whole fearing God thing, and loving people . . . I mean . . . is that what you're talking about, Jesus?

"I'm just not sure we can do it."

To which Jesus replies, "Don't worry. I'm sending something to help you out and this thing is called the spirit of truth or the breath of God (That same breath that he tied into wind earlier.)

She's[139] coming and she'll *walk* through this with you and *empower* you. She will *remind* you of all the things that I've said and she will *teach* you. I'm not leaving you alone. I leave you peace and her. Don't let your hearts be troubled and certainly, if nothing else, don't be afraid. This is going to be awesome.

She will walk with us.
She will empower us.
She will remind us of the way to live.
She will teach us.

Of course, we'll figure out things like "slavery might be wrong" because Jesus said she will continue to teach us things beyond the menu.

Of course, we'll be able to love—like that—because she will enable us to see the world differently.

Of course, we shouldn't be afraid or troubled or worry because she is with us and she is from God and she will enable us to do greater things.

Of course, it makes sense why Jesus told people to stop studying the Bible to find life and start tasting, drinking, and living Jesus for life.[140]

There are some who read these words and may be getting nervous or afraid at this point. These are "fine lines" I have often heard. And we're generally afraid of "fine lines".

"Fines lines" are difficult. They are everywhere.

There are fine lines between laziness and patience. How do we know when we are waiting for something to happen and when we are just sitting around?

There are fine lines between naiveté and faith. How do we know when we are expecting something to happen that will never happen, when we are ignorant, or when we are simply acting in faith?

There are fine lines between justification and clarification. How do we know when we know what to do and are trying to make something else happen versus just trying to figure out what to do?

But the idea of teaching *beyond* the Bible really scares some people because it's a fine line between teachings and new ideas and heresy. There are fine lines between what *we* do and what God supposedly does, and I get that.

So I acknowledge the lines are fine. I'm alright with that. Maybe we can just end it this way because I find this whole idea of spirit and empowerment to be integral to the Christian faith.

I saw this post on Facebook recently:

> False gospels are seductive because they always tell you that you are more righteous than you are and have more power than you possess.

This seems so confusing. Is this statement saying that the real good news is that we are worse than we think and that we possess less power than we think? What in the world is *good* about that?

And yet, this is what is often communicated.

Somehow, the message of God to us, of Jesus to his disciples—the revolutionary, amazing, beautiful, inspiring, hopeful, empowering, enchanting, good message of God—has been replaced by a mundane, depressing, counterfeit, empty, and just plain bad message along these lines:

> Guys, I'm leaving. Be afraid. Be very afraid. It's going to be rough. And it's going to be rough because once I leave this world . . . well, things are going to get uglier than they already are. You'll be alone, and we know what that means for the planet. I mean, someday I'll return, flying through the clouds with lightning bolts and stuff, but until then . . . well, your chances of dying before that are much better, so basically just wait to die. While you're waiting, don't dream, don't imagine, don't create, and don't pursue big things. I mean, that's God's work. Keep your head down. Do what everyone else does: go to church a little, numb yourself with whatever works, get a job (for some money), and tell people how great your religion is. Some will live pretty well, but most will live a crappy life because God's plan is to make you something great in heaven when you die. So, until then, try not to screw up too bad. Although, you probably will because . . . what else are you going to do? You're just a stupid human.

When employees are hired at Apple, they supposedly get a letter, and it goes something like this:

> There's work and there's your life's work.
>
> The kind of work that has your fingerprints all over it. The kind of work that you'd never compromise on. That you'd sacrifice a weekend for. You can do that kind of work at Apple. People don't come here to play it safe. They come here to swim in the deep end.
>
> They want their work to add up to something. Something big. Something that couldn't happen anywhere else.

Welcome to Apple.

What a computer company tells its employees is better than what many people think God tells humanity.

Something is wrong with this picture.

There is a book written by Steven Pressfield called *The War of Art*. I've read it multiple times because it's one of *those* books. It always inspires and maybe never as much as the final paragraph of the book.

> Are you a born writer? Were you put here on earth to be a painter, a scientist, an apostle of peace? In the end the question can only be answered by action.
>
> Do it or don't do it.
>
> It may help to think of it this way. If you were meant to cure cancer or write a symphony or crack cold fusion and you don't do it, you not only hurt yourself, even destroy yourself. You hurt your children. You hurt me. You hurt the planet.
>
> You shame the angels who watch over you and you spite the Almighty, who created you and only you with your unique gifts, for the sole purpose of nudging the human race one millimeter farther along its path back to God.
>
> Creative work is not a selfish act or a bid for attention on the part of the actor. It's a gift to the world and every being in it. Don't cheat us of your contribution. Give us what you've got.[141]

If the message you have received from Christianity, God, Jesus, faith, spirituality, is closer to the first two messages than the last two, then I do have good news for you.

You've heard the wrong message, and it only keeps getting better.

fourteen

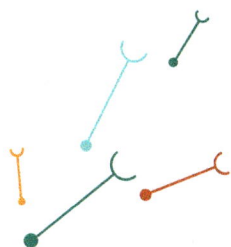

rise.

William Kamkwamba was a 14-year-old living in Malawi. His family and others around him were surviving on only one meal a day. Malawi had been through a severe drought seven years earlier and had still not truly recovered. His father, a farmer, had no crops to work and couldn't supply any food.

William was kicked out of school because he could not afford the $80 for tuition, so he started to spend his days at the local library. One day, a picture of a windmill caught his eye and he decided to build one. Wind, in addition to despair and poverty, was one thing he had all around him.

William started combing through junkyards and collecting old bicycle parts, tractor parts, batteries, plastic pipes—whatever he could find. He made a screwdriver out of a corncob and a nail. Everyone called him crazy, possessed, and mad. They laughed at him, his intentions, and his dreams.

But he kept going. William says he couldn't wait to finish that windmill: "I wanted to finish it just to prove them wrong. I knew people would then stop thinking I was crazy."

Eventually, William completed his first windmill and even powered a light bulb with it. William proceeded to build several other windmills, each of them generating electricity and enabling people to pump water, charge phones, listen to radios, and to have light.

William went on to the African Leadership Academy in Johannesburg, South Africa, and spoke at a TED Conference[142] where he shared his story. As of this writing, William is studying at Dartmouth University and close to graduating.

Dwayne Allen was a kid from the wrong side of the tracks. Growing up without a father, he attended an alternative school and had numerous brushes with the law and school authorities, including multiple suspensions.

One day in the school hallway, Dwayne was approached by Wayne Inman, the high school football coach. Coach Inman asked if Dwayne played football. When Dwayne replied that he did not, Coach Inman gave him $10 and told him something like, "You can buy a bag of dope or get yourself a physical and come out for football."

Dwayne says that day changed his life.

He went out for football and ended up being coached, in more ways than one, by Inman. Coach Inman became a father-figure to Dwayne.

Dwayne went on to play football at Clemson University, where he was drafted by the Indianapolis Colts in 2012. That year, with Andrew Luck throwing him the ball, he started every game and helped the Colts turn around their season and make the playoffs.[143]

Agustin is an elderly gentleman who lives in Honduras. If you want to fall in love with someone in a video, watch the documentary *Everything is Incredible*.[144]

As a child, Agustin was diagnosed with polio. But that didn't stop him from chasing his dream of becoming a pilot. He spent some time repairing shoes (sometimes giving them away) and grew up with an alcoholic brother who would shout out to everyone that he may be the alcoholic brother, but at least he wasn't the crazy one. In 1958, Agustin began building a helicopter.

Agustin has now spent over 50 years building a helicopter out of random parts that he finds at the local dump all while being stuck in a wheelchair. He says, "For everyone it's been a case of mockery because the whole world thinks that it is impossible."

As far as I know, he is still working on his helicopter and has not yet flown it. Agustin says, "The problem is that everything is incredible and people don't accept it."[145]

There is something inspirational about all three of these stories. Something moving. Something beautiful. And while they are all inspirational, they are not the same.

Two of them deal with people making the most out of what little they have. Finding life.

Two are successful, as generally defined by most of the world (one playing in the NFL and the other speaking at a TED Conference), and one is still trying.

Two were called crazy, told they were out of their mind and were mocked incessantly by others. One of them is still mocked today. They all have experienced, or are still experiencing, tremendous pain.

One of them had someone walk alongside of him, walk through pain with him, and love him. The other two were alone in their quests.

But there is a common theme in all three stories and, actually, this theme is in *every* good story whether it's a movie, television show, novel, etc. Someone overcame obstacles. Someone fought through the pain and forces against them. Someone went against the odds and came out victorious on the other side.

Someone rose above.

Seth Godin has a book titled *The Dip*. Mr. Godin basically says that "the Dip" affects everything we do: business, art, creativity, religion, etc.:

> Almost everything in life worth doing is controlled by the Dip.
>
> The Dip is the long slog between starting and mastery. A long slog that's actually a shortcut, because it gets you where you want to go faster than any other path.
>
> The Dip is the combination of bureaucracy and busywork you must deal with in order to get certified in scuba diving.

> The Dip is the difference between the easy "beginner" technique and the more useful "expert" approach in skiing or fashion design.
>
> The Dip is the long stretch between beginner's luck and real accomplishment.
>
> The Dip is the set of artificial screens set up to keep people like you out.[146]

He calls it "the Dip" because it's when our results no longer match our effort. While they often do in the beginning, eventually everything reaches that point where the results fall, even though the effort continues.

But . . .

> Successful people don't just ride out the Dip. They don't just buckle down and survive it. No, they lean into the Dip. They push harder, changing the rules as they go. Just because you know you're in the Dip doesn't mean you have to live happily with it. Dips don't last quite as long when you whittle at them.[147]

The Dip doesn't stay. Even though many people quit while in the Dip, the best keep going. They ride it out, and they come out on the other side.

William fought through the Dip. As did Dwayne. And Agustin is fighting, or already has, depending on your perspective.

If there is a word to describe coming out of the Dip—the part when the results begin to match the effort, and maybe even move beyond it—it's the word "rise."

Rise.

Which reminds me of my favorite movie of 2012: *The Dark Knight Rises*.

Batman is my favorite superhero because he's just a normal guy—a normal guy with an insane amount of money, access to technology and weapons unlike any other person, and an uncanny ability to dodge bullets, heal from wounds, etc., but he's still just a normal guy. He can be defeated without the use of green, alien rock (like Superman's Kryptonite), and doesn't have superhuman abilities like Spider-Man. He can fall, and when he does, he falls hard.

The Dark Knight Rises is about Batman's fall. In the movie, Bruce Wayne (Batman's true identity) is older, frailer, and he's been defeated. He finds himself in a prison, a literal pit (or Dip), where only one person has ever escaped—a child.

Bruce tries to escape, but can't. He has to climb out of the pit and make a considerable leap from one rock to another so he ties a rope around himself in case he falls, which he continues to do. He falls every time, and he can't get out of the Dip.

There's a great scene where another prisoner, who happens to be blind, begins to talk to Bruce about his escape attempt.

> Prisoner: You do not fear death. You think this makes you strong. It makes you weak.
>
> Bruce Wayne: Why?
>
> Prisoner: How can you move faster than possible, fight longer than possible without the most powerful impulse of the spirit: the fear of death?
>
> Bruce Wayne: I do fear death. I fear dying in here, while my city burns, and there's no one there to save it.
>
> Prisoner: Then make the climb.
>
> Bruce Wayne: How?
>
> Prisoner: As the child did. Without the rope. Then fear will find you again.

So Bruce begins to make the climb without the rope.

The music kicks in, and the prisoners begin to chant *dey-shey bah-sur-rah*, which translates to "he rises." The tension builds and the anticipation is thick (even though we all know what's going to happen). Then Bruce jumps and finally makes the leap to the rock and rises out of the pit.

It's inspiring, just like William, Dwayne, and Agustin's stories.

A doctor who had been treating patients from the Boston Marathon bombing was on the news and said, "The more they are challenged, the more they rise" in reference to his fellow surgeons and staff.

I got chills hearing that.

All of these stories are inspiring because they remind us that we, too, can rise. We all have our Dips and no matter where we are within, we, too, can rise out of them.

We can come out on the other side.

This brings us to another "rise" story. Arguably, it should be the most inspiring "rise" story of them all. It's the ultimate Dip and the ultimate rise. It should be the most inspirational and powerful Dip and rise of *any* story.

But, it's usually not. I'm talking about what happens right after Jesus tells his disciples that they will do greater things: he dies, and then he rises.

And yet, most people are more inspired by a man who builds windmills than the story of Jesus rising from the dead. I get chills on my neck when I see Bruce Wayne rise out of the pit, yet I rarely do when I talk about Jesus coming out of a grave.

Why is that?

Sure, it's the music. Sure, it's the technology. Sure, it's more real to see a movie than read a story. But really? Is that it?

I think it's bigger than that.

I think we have taken the story and . . .

> domesticated
> minimized
> misunderstood
> separated out
> rationalized
> sterilized
> neutralized
> neutered

> and *lost* the story.

We've taken some of the greatest parts of the story and removed them, making the story incredibly . . . weak. Andrew Stanton, who has played a part in writing every *Pixar* film, says, "The best stories infuse a sense of wonder." I wonder if we've taken all the wonder out of the greatest story ever told. We've taken a mysterious, wonderful story and reduced it to something like:

> God loves humans, but God is bound by justice and holiness so God can't really love humans unless there is some kind of payment. So God becomes God's own payment so that God can love us again, as long as we accept the love; otherwise, the God who loves us will torture us forever.

That's just not a good story. It's a terrible story.

Maybe we can look at the story again? The *whole* story.

The story begins with a poem about a garden, which is a pretty harmless way to start a story. I don't think the story is meant to be taken literally but I do think the story is meant to inspire us.

I don't know if it was *just* a garden. In fact, my guess is that it wasn't.

Interestingly enough, researchers have spent a lot of time trying to figure out the most common landscape that invokes beauty for the most people in the world. (Researchers truly do research everything.) They found one, and it happened to be something very similar to how that original landscape in that poem is described: birds, trees, nearby water, and diverse greenery.[148]

Whatever that garden was, I believe it was beautiful. In *every* sense.

The landscape also had a man and a woman and animals and fruits and vegetables and it was described as good.

There is a God in the story. The God is also good. In every way. The God takes chaos and creates some kind of order out of it. And the results are the garden and the man and the woman and the fruit.

So things are good. In the same way that *whoa*, *palah*, gazing up at the stars, and looking at a newborn baby are good.

The God is love in the way that the wedding passage talks about love. This means that the God loves everyone—not just some people in the garden and not just people who do everything right—but *all* people. That love continues throughout the story, although sometimes it's harder to see than other times, but it's always there.

The God is also just. Unfortunately, people hear that and they think of justice in the way that we think of justice: punishment for a crime. While that is a *form* of justice, it's not the form of justice that this God is all about, at least not in my opinion (and that of many others). This kind of justice is under a canopy of love and this kind of justice is not about retribution and violence, but about restoration and healing because that's how love always works.

This justice is always about fixing things. For *all* people.

Since this God is all about love—the overriding principle of this God—this God allows freedom because without freedom there cannot be love. This God could have had power and control—even robots!—but I don't think that's what this God wanted.

The humans start to make decisions that are not good, because they can. It all starts with their desire to know more. To understand. To gain wisdom. They start to make decisions that cause pain to themselves, to others, to the world, and to God. Yes, this God feels pain, too.

That quest for wisdom and knowledge, begins a journey of pain. It often does.

There are wars, there are disagreements, and there are people who claim to do things in the name of God because they "heard from God" even though those things are not good. And not loving. And not like Jesus.

Which should cause us to wonder if they were really what God wanted.

Others, often called prophets, come along and try to correct mistakes. They say lots of astounding things about religious festivals, sacrifices, prayer, fasting, and how God sometimes can't stand these religious things (even that God hates them) because that's not what this God is all about.

Others, often more prophets, in the story try to remind people that this God is about blessing the world. Fixing the world. Healing the world. Bringing justice, in that sense, to the world. This God is about sharing resources and taking care of people who are poor, oppressed, or unfortunate, and giving them something good.

This makes perfect sense when we remember that this all started in a garden that was good, and *that* was what God wanted.

Contained within this larger story are hundreds of smaller stories of a God who is trying in a variety of ways to move humanity back toward the garden. But since this God always works *within* cultures, languages, wrong concepts of the God, concepts of *other* gods, as well as anger, revenge, justification and, often, just plain ignorance and selfishness, the task is difficult.

Just like today.

Much of the story is about a big Dip for humanity, especially for the people who claimed to follow this God. It wasn't working. They find themselves as slaves, then they are freed, then they take slaves of their own, then they find themselves as slaves again . . . it's confusing and sad and tragic and painful.

There is confusion and drama and more pain.

So this God decides to come to Earth in the form of the very creatures that were in that garden. The story says that this God, who was everything, took on the form of a human, and became nothing.

At first glance, that's a little insulting. But you must remember our place in the universe and the potential for infinite universes and then imagine a higher power, that is as big as those universes, becoming human, like you and me.

Well, the word "nothing" works fine. It's overwhelming and hard to fathom.

But love is like that sometimes.

Jesus is born from a woman. A human woman. He lives in her uterus, enters the world, and takes his first breath, and starts to grow like all humans. Jesus eventually walks, talks, and says he's here to clear up much of that confusion over what God looks like, how God acts, and what God would do. He's here to make it as clear as possible. Or maybe better said, he's here to make the things that should be clear as clear as possible and not worry about the other things. There are still many mysteries.

Apparently, though, enough is pretty clear because people really don't like what they hear. They have other views of God that are more powerful and violent and controlling and, well, this Jesus really doesn't tell it that way.

> When the pain gets so bad that you're ready to quit, you've set yourself up as someone with nothing to lose. And someone with nothing to lose has quite a bit of power. You can go for broke. Challenge authority. Attempt unattempted alternatives. Lean

into a problem; lean so far that you might just lean right through it.[149]

Jesus does just that. Jesus challenges authority, attempts unattempted alternatives, and leans into the problem . . . with everything he has. Jesus goes through his own Dip, which means this God, who has given up everything in some mysterious sense, falls.

God falls?

Ponder that for a moment. The biggest, baddest, most powerful force in the universe . . . falls. That means the next time we fall and we raise our fist to God and say, "Do you know what's happening to me down here? How did you let me fall like this?" God might reply with something like, "Do you know *my* story?"

So Jesus, who says, "If you've seen me, you've seen God" dies.

Nietzsche was *almost* right. God *did* die.

To those who were following the story at the time, it was over. God lost. Jesus was dead. The Dip won. All accounts say that any idea of Jesus rising were nonsense, and the people who had been closest to him were downcast, wondering, doubtful, afraid, disappointed, crying, and frustrated.

They thought it was over. They felt like we usually do during Dips, and that Dip was overwhelming.

This forces us to stop for a moment because most of the theological theories for Jesus *needing* to die would *still* work if the story had ended there. That means no one should have been downcast, wondering, doubtful, afraid, disappointed, crying, or frustrated.

Just in case you weren't aware, there are, at least, seven theories as to why Jesus had to die and what the cross symbolized. Yes, *theories*. Satisfaction Theory, Ransom Theory, Christus Victor Theory, Moral Exemplar Theory, Last Scapegoat Theory, Satisfaction Theory, and Solidarity Theory. Arguably the most popular theory in Western Protestantism, and definitely evangelicalism, is the *Penal Substitution Theory*. This theory says Jesus died on the cross for our sins. Penal refers to the punishment of offenders under the legal system. So something had to be paid, and God punished himself in order to be able to love humans.

With all of these theories, we must remember: "The god whose existence is proven and disproven by academicians is rarely the god anyone actually believes in."[150] They do, of course, affect us, but there are deeper, more personal and human questions to consider: If Jesus *had* to *die* for our sins, then why did he *rise*?

Was the rise just frosting on the cake?

If our view of the story ends there and no rise is necessary than many of us who find ourselves stuck in the Dip might as well stay. Sometimes life sucks and then we die.

But that can't be the story, right? That can't be everything?

It's not.

Jesus came out of the Dip. Jesus rises because he *had* to. If he doesn't rise, theological implications ensue. Paul says that if Jesus doesn't rise, people who believe in him should be pitied more than anyone else. (Which means if your theory of doesn't demand a rise, there might be something wrong with it.)

There are story implications as well. If Jesus doesn't rise, then where's the inspiration and the power? Frankly, if God couldn't rise, how am I supposed to?

There are all kinds of things to take from this powerful story, but there are two main points as they relate to what we've been talking about.

The first is that wherever we are—in pain, in life, in the Dip, on the rise, about to enter another dip, or somewhere in-between—God is with us.

Eli Wiesel, while watching a child hang from the gallows at Auschwitz, hears someone say, "For God's sake, where is God?" He writes, "I hear a voice answer, 'Where is He? This is where, hanging here from this gallows.'"[151]

The child hanging on the gallows, the newborn baby that doesn't make it, the tears of a mother who just lost her child at a race, the comfort of a stranger to that mother . . . No matter where we're at, God is *there*. (This just happens to be one of the centerpieces of the Solidarity Theory, and one of the reasons I'm so drawn to it.)

This is a story of a God, who is good, who is full of love, and who prompts restoration to that garden, who gives it all up and becomes a servant of love in order to say:

I love you. I'm there with you right now. I will do anything to make sure you know that I love you and that I always have.

This is a God who is in complete solidarity with all the pain of the island we live on:

> He enters into an elementary school and murders innocent children.
>
> She discovers she has stage four cancer at the age of 27.
>
> He decides to take a nap in the afternoon and never wakes up, leaving his wife and children with no chance to say goodbye.
>
> The debt piles up, the car accident happens, and he is still single even though he wants nothing more in life than to find a partner.
>
> He still can't forgive himself for what he did to those innocent people in the Vietnamese village.
>
> The loneliness gets so thick and heavy that it's hard to function.
>
> She dates him for two years and believes he's "the one" only to find out he has found someone else.
>
> She can't get pregnant no matter what they try or how much money they spend.

The divorce comes after 23 years of marriage, and it comes via a text message.

They pick up the shattered hearts and emotions of the kids and try to put them back together.

This God is not here to *cause* the pain or to *watch* the pain, but just to *be* there with us through it all.

This also means that this God does not take sides. God is not on the side of the attacker in a "just war" any more than God is on the side of those who are attacked out of a "just war theory." God is not on the side of those who torture any more than God is on the side of those who are tortured. To drive the point further, God is not just on *your* side or *our* side whenever there are sides. God is on the side of our enemies. God is on the side of the opressed. God is always on the side of those who are hurt and in pain, wherever they are, and however they got there because that is what God does to show love. And that is how God's love operates.

There is no other option.

That is not how most of us usually imagine God—a God who is on the side of our enemies, those we torture, those we oppress, those we harm, and those whom we think we are better than. No more formulas, idols, and abuses of power here.

This God, who is with us, who is all about love, who has faith in humanity and in our role to love others and help them rise, expects us to also be with *them* in their pain.

> *Two are better than one, because they have a good return for their labor: If either of them falls down, one can help the other up. But pity anyone who falls and has no one to help them up. Also, if two lie down together, they will keep warm. But how can one keep warm alone? Though one may be overpowered, two can defend themselves. A cord of three strands is not quickly broken.*[152]

This passage is also frequently read at weddings, but, again, it's so much bigger and better and enthralling.

This passage is talking about faith. This is community. This is caring for one another. This is rejoicing with those who rejoice and mourning with those who mourn. This is what it's all about.

I once told a young girl, who said she was lonely, to go find a church. I said if she went to a church and did not find someone to help her in some way with her loneliness, to stand with her in some kind of solidarity, then she should go to another church until she found a church that did.

Being a pastor, it made me nervous to say this to her since I know there have been lonely people who have come to church, and have left.

Although it might hurt, it's the truth. Nobody should go through pain alone. Nobody. Dr. Abraham Verghese makes this beautiful statement regarding pain and comfort:

> When you suffer enough, what you want especially in addition to your best technology, best chemo, you also want a caring, empathetic physician who really expresses concern for you. And I think that aspect is why I came up with that phrase, that the most important innovation in the next decade will be recognizing the power of the human hand. Not just to diagnose, but to comfort, to reassure, and to say, I will walk this path with you to the end of the line. I'll be with you.[153]

I'll be with you. I will walk this path with you, human to human, believing that God is with us as well saying the same thing with us.

It might be the most important *idea* in human history. But . . .

It *still* can't end there, right? If that's it, then we're all stuck in the pain with no way out and *still*, no reason for Jesus to rise.

We have all kinds of phrases for when we're going through the Dip:

"You've got to keep fighting."

"It takes a while to turn the ship around."

"It takes time."

All of these deal with some kind of momentum. When Andre Agassi was in his Dip and decided he was going to do something to get out of it, once and for all, he wrote this:

> Our best intentions are often thwarted by external forces—forces that we ourselves set in motion long ago. Decisions, especially bad ones, create their own kind of momentum, and momentum can be a pain to stop, as every athlete knows. Even when we vow to change, even when we sorrow and atone for our mistakes, the momentum of our past keeps carrying us down the wrong road. Momentum rules the world. Momentum says: Hold on, not so fast, I'm still running things here. As a friend likes to say, quoting an old Greek poem: The minds of the everlasting gods are not changed suddenly.[154]

We've all been there.

The momentum of the past. It's there, pushing us to where we don't want to go. Momentum does seem to rule the world. The minds of the gods don't suddenly change. Momentum seems to even rule them.

And if we just hear parts of the ultimate rise story, the idea of momentum might be one of the most depressing ideas around. But, if we hear the *entire* story, it might be one of the most encouraging ideas around.

Because *this* story is all about momentum and the momentum is to rise.

The momentum *is* overcoming.

The momentum gets us through whatever it is, wherever we are in the Dip, and *to* some place better.

The momentum is to *rise*.

This is the story and always has been. This is the trajectory of this God— to get humanity back to where it's good—and it has never changed. This God has always fought, and is still fighting, to get back to good.

This God is not only in the Dip with us, this God is in the bottom of the Dip with all the momentum of the universe and all the power of love and restoration to get us out of the Dip and to someplace better.

To a place where we are alive again.

This God paints a picture of the future—of where we can go—and pulls us there with the momentum of the universe, which makes our past and puny momentum—which was taking us where we don't want to go—fade away.

This rise is not about delaying the inevitable. Jesus didn't rise to die again. Jesus rose to defeat the Dip and all the Dips around.

That's got some power.

Ever since my son and I watched *The Dark Knight* last summer, we have this little thing we say to each other. We say "rise."

> So, if he's on the football field and drops the ball: *rise.*

> If he's on the lacrosse field and misses the hit: *rise.*

> If he's struggling with homework: *rise.*

> If he's wrestling around with a friend and gets pinned down: *rise.*

He does the same for me.

> If I get a nasty email from someone: *rise.*

> If I don't feel like any of it is coming together for a new project: *rise.*

> If my ankle is hurting and I don't think I can run: *rise.*

It's becoming our family motto.

To rise *is* the story's message.

Jesus rises and says, "Repentance for the forgiveness of sins will be preached in his name to all nations, beginning at Jerusalem."[155] This statement is packed with religious terminology that gets twisted around and manipulated.

But, said more plainly, some of us are stuck in pain that we've inflicted on ourselves, or others, and we need to get out of the Dip and rise to a place where we become something better and new and transformed.

Jesus said I'm here to do that. I've risen to tell you it can happen. To you. There's power here in *this* love.

Paul says that whole Jesus story applies to us, too. We were dead and buried and have been raised from the dead so that we might have new life.[156]

Right here, right now. New *life*.

If you're stuck in a Dip with the actions that have caused pain and you can't quite get out of it, acknowledge your mistakes and tell shame to go to hell, because God says you're better than that. And God is in the Dip with you, ready to haul you out and bring you into the current of the universe and to a new and transformed and inspiring life.

Rise.

There are too many people who think they are not enough. They are not worthy enough. They can't be a good enough husband, wife, father, mother, son, daughter, friend, boss, boyfriend, girlfriend—whatever it is, the failure is too big. The mistake is too large to overcome. The Dip is too deep. The shame is too thick.

But this is a story of a God who says "me, too." It's a story of a God who says, "We'll do greater things because I believe in you and because you *are* enough and because I love you and because I'm there with you in whatever Dip of shame you're in. I'll pull you out and change your world."

Don't believe what everyone else says. Believe what I say.

Believe *that*. Rise.

If you have cancer . . .

If you were abused by your father, your priest, your pastor, or your friend . . .

If you are going through a divorce . . .

If you are struggling with financial debt . . .

If you just told your parents you are gay and your parents want nothing to do with you . . .

If you just lost your father . . .

If you just lost a friend . . .

If you are addicted to alcohol, drugs, sex, or anything else to numb the pain of reality . . .

If you just lost your job . . .

If you're bored . . .

If you're jealous . . .

If you can't forgive . . .

If you're a cynic . . .

If you're struggling with your kids and wondering what to do . . .

If you're never satisfied . . .

If you always feel like you need more . . .

If you don't know if your marriage is going to make it . . .

If you don't know how you're going to tell her that secret . . .

If your name is on an arrest warrant . . .

If you don't think it will ever get better . . .

Rise.

God is with you in the Dip, no matter how deep or large or long, and God is hugging you, comforting you, and telling you that love is the ultimate power and motivation of the universe. And this God has an infinite amount of love for you, and this love and this God and this story are pulling you to someplace beautiful and beyond your wildest dreams.

It's *mysterious* and *palah* and *whoa* and *right now*.

Too many of us live in a world of black and white and dull gray. It's an insipid world filled with dull, boring, and bland Dips. Let this God smash in, opening up rays of color and vibrancy, vitality and life, of love and mercy and grace and momentum, because there is a love that is stronger than any evil in this world, and it simply will not be defeated.

This love, quite simply, can't die. Start living with it and see where it takes you.

I think there is a reason that William, Dwayne, and Agustin inspire us and make us smile. They are more than an inspiration. They are an insight into a force of the universe—a momentum to rise. They are an insight into God.

They are reminders of what this story is all about—that we can do greater things, that we can rise, that there is a God who is pulling the world somewhere and that somewhere is good and better and where we want to go.

They make us smile. because they make God smile, especially when we see God in them and acknowledge them for what they are.[157]

This story is a grand one.

Rise.

fifteen

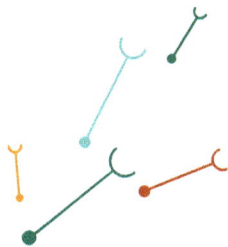

breakfast.

The story keeps going.

Doesn't it always?

It starts in the evening.[158] After his death, Jesus has appeared to some people, but he isn't around when seven of his disciples are hanging out and Peter says, "I'm going fishing."

Jesus has just risen from the dead and they are going fishing. It seems pretty normal because sometimes it is, just like Solomon said. We've just seen one of the biggest "rise" stories come out of one of the biggest "Dip" stories, and the disciples are going fishing because they are hungry.

They fish all night and catch nothing. If I fish for a few hours and catch nothing, I'm pretty frustrated. I can't imagine what I would look like if I had been in their shoes. And fishing is their job, their livelihood, their food source, and much more important than having a cool photo of a big fish to post on Instagram.

Early in the morning when the air still smells clean and crisp and the sun is just peeking up over the horizon, a man appears on the shore. He calls out to the disciples in the boat and says, "Friends, haven't you any fish?"

Friends is actually the Greek word for "children." So maybe it was more of a: "Hey, boys! No fish out there?" or "Hey, kids! Trouble fishing?" But no matter how you translate it, it's got a little bit of an edge to it. Jesus seems to be a little more playful than in the past, and I mean this honestly. I would imagine he is. The worst is over. He did it. There's nothing to dread or worry about anymore, which in this case was an incredibly monumental important *something*.

He's won. You've got to think he's feeling pretty good about it.

So . . . "Hey, boys! No fish?"

Then he tells them (and they still don't know who he is) to throw their nets over the right side of the boat because they will find some fish over there. You would assume that they had already done that, right? At some point in the night? But they do it again and they end up catching too many fish and can't haul them all in. Fish, fish, everywhere fish.

Then they finally recognize that it's Jesus who was talking to them. Peter jumps into the water and starts running toward the shoreline (it wasn't very deep) while the other six disciples tow in the massive haul of fish and tell Peter, "No worries, Peter. We'll haul in all of this fish even though it was your idea to fish in the first place."

They haul in the fish (apparently there was 153 in total) and they find Jesus sitting on the beach with a small, coal fire and some fish already cooking. Where he got *his* fish, we don't know.

But we do know that he says, "Come and have some breakfast."

Let's eat.

So the Jesus who has risen from the dead is sitting on a beach with some guys, stoking a fire, and eating fish for breakfast?

It's so . . . normal.

Dips and rises, fears and desires, idols and formulas, mystery and futures, letting go and building up, humanity and God . . . sometimes it's just eating breakfast with some friends on a lakeside shore at sunrise because that is as sacred of a moment as sacred moments get.

Which is what Solomon has been telling us all along, right?

If we can start to take the ordinary acts of eating a breakfast, fishing, cooking, hauling in nets, and see them for the moments they are, then we start to open the box of God, of formula, of fear, of desire, and of life.

We no longer go to God in a temple to be holy, we make the moment holy by acknowledging that God is already here, and this moment is as sacred and full of significance and holiness as we can find.

The whole story of Jesus is so ordinarily extraordinary that it twists everything upside down. Is this how God, who becomes human, really acts? He just does normal stuff sometimes?

We're often so busy looking for the spiritual, angelic beings that we miss Jesus. That we miss God. In fact, after the resurrection, people were doing this all over the place. Mary is at the tomb, and she's talking to angels and ignoring the "gardener" behind her. He's too normal. Couldn't be him.

The gardener was Jesus.

The disciples are walking along on a road and talking to Jesus for a long time before they recognize him. Surely he wouldn't return and just talk to us while walking on a road, they wonder. He'd be flying around or something, right?

And even in this story, he shows up on the shore and the disciples don't recognize him. They've already seen him and, again, they don't know if it's him. Maybe he looked different or maybe they expected him to look different because people who have been dead for three days and then are resurrected don't just walk on a beach and cook breakfast.

Or maybe they do.

We often miss sacred moments of life because we're so busy looking at things that are yelling and screaming and shouting how holy and god-ly they are that we overlook the truly miraculous things we should be paying attention to.

Sometimes . . .

> going to school . . .

> washing the car . . .

> building a fence . . .

mowing the lawn . . .

riding a dirt bike . . .

going to a lacrosse game . . .

listening to a song . . .

eating dinner . . .

sitting at a desk with a laptop . . .

going skiing . . .

fixing a car . . .

and going on a bike ride . . .

. . . are what it looks like to rise and live.

What's potentially even more amazing about this story, and the other stories of this Jesus who rose, are all the things that Jesus *doesn't* bother to talk about.

Jesus, who was dead for three days, didn't come back and tell us that he descended into hell and fought the devil. He didn't tell us he went to hell at all. He didn't tell us he went to heaven or, if he did, what it was like.

He didn't talk about what comes after this life.

This is astounding. Jesus, comes back from death and doesn't tell us everything he knows? Yet, in this day and age, books about heaven and hell fill the best seller lists.

Keeping with the wisdom of Solomon, Jesus focuses all his attention on *now*. Right this moment. Not *thens* and *somedays*.

He talks about how to pass along these whoa stories, about how to live and tell others to live, about sharing the good news of freedom and liberation and says: "Don't be afraid" and "Peace" and "I'm hungry." He says, "Receive her," the holy spirit and that we can forgive sins. He says "It's me; touch my side" and "The fishing is better over there." He says, "Feed my sheep, follow me, stop worrying about the future, and stop worrying about everyone else and just follow me."

It's amazing how much drama surrounds heaven and hell within Christian circles.

Who will go to heaven?

Who will go to hell?

What do they look like?

How do we get to heaven?

How will we know who will and won't get to heaven?

Let's not forget all of the name calling of heretics and false prophets and warnings of wolves in sheep's clothing and so much of it is related to heaven and hell.

And let's not forget the one person who could have told us the answers to all of those questions and to all of the mysteries of the afterlife . . .

Didn't.

Instead, he ate breakfast.

What does *that* say?

Jesus seems much more concerned with whether there is life before death than whether there is life after death—which, once again, is exactly what Solomon has been saying all along.

sixteen

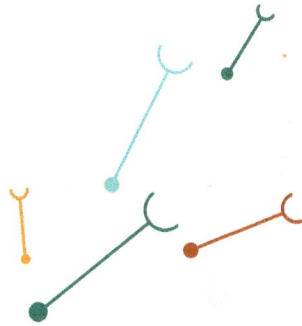

waves, vectors, you.

Those disciples, who were fishing all night long, working their butts off while nothing was happening, remind us of something else to be aware of. After all of their hard work, Jesus comes along and tells them to fish on the right side of the boat and . . . suddenly they have more fish than they can imagine. Suddenly what they have been trying to do all night, is happening, more than they could have imagined.

I've surfed once in my life. I'm obviously no expert. At all. But I've watched enough surfers, talked with enough surfers, and learned a few things. Plus, you only need one experience to learn something valuable.

Surfing is a lot of work. It's exhausting. My arms were ready to fall off when I was done. It takes a ton of effort. But, it also takes something else: waves. And it doesn't matter how much effort a surfer puts into surfing; if there is no wave, there will be no surfing. It won't work. And no one controls the waves.

They happen or they don't.

So you have work and waves, and they have to combine, just right, to make something magical happen. I think this is important as we talk about rising and living and changing the world.

Sometimes we work really hard all night only to find that there are no fish. We're exhausted.

Sometimes we spend all of our time paddling to get up on the board and we don't. It's not very fun.

Sometimes we force things to happen because we think that things are supposed to happen all the time. But maybe they aren't supposed to happen.

At times, we just need to sit out on the ocean, look at the sun, and wait. Maybe catch a tan. Maybe chat with friends. Maybe just do nothing because there is nothing that needs to be done.

Sometimes the waves start to come. Sometimes you cast your net on the right side of the boat and, suddenly, whoa! What happened? This thing is blowing up and growing, so what do we do now?

It's not time to sit and watch. It's time to paddle.

When we started our church, I often told people, "I'm just riding the wave" because that's what it felt like. Although I knew something had happened, I didn't exactly know what, and I knew I was working hard, but it was also fun and exciting and exhilarating.

We caught that baby and we were cruising.

Other times we feel like we missed it. The wave passed. We feel like we'll never catch another one. We had our shot and we blew it. We'll never get the opportunity to do that again.

I have good news for you. The waves *always* come. There will be more. The worst thing we can do is start paddling like crazy and standing on a board to try and *make* it happen. After experiencing failures, you just need to relax, wait, and look.

Waves are *always* coming.

There's even more good news.

Remember when Peter jumped out of the boat and ran toward Jesus? Well, before he did that, he had an interesting encounter with Jesus. Before Jesus died, he told all of the disciples that they would reject him and act like they didn't know him when he returned. Jesus told them they would all lie in order to save their own skin.

Peter was pretty upset with this and told Jesus that he would never, ever, ever do such a thing. He said that he would die with Jesus if he had to.

It turns out Jesus was right and Peter was wrong.

Three times Peter adamantly denied that he ever knew Jesus. And he made sure people knew this. He even swore it with an oath and called down curses on people and swore at people who asked if he knew Jesus. Peter made sure that no one thought for a second that he had ever hung out with Jesus.[159]

I don't know if you've ever been betrayed. If so, you know how Jesus felt. Better yet, Jesus knows how you feel.

I don't know if you've ever been the one who promised someone that you would never let them down. Ever. And then you did. It hurts. It stings. It's painful.

I don't know if you've ever promised God something and then went back on it. I don't know if you've ever gone from "I'll die with you" to calling down curses on someone who asked if you ever knew God, but if so, Peter knows exactly how you feel.

Peter went outside and wept bitterly when he realized he had been wrong and Jesus had been right. We've all been there.

It feels like missing a wave.

Back to that beach. We're there having breakfast with Jesus, and he looks at Peter and says, "Do you love me?" He asks Peter three times.

What's interesting is that Jesus asks Peter if he loves him like Jesus loves Peter. While English has only one word for "love," Greek—the language this story was written in—has four different words to describe four different types of love: a sexual love, a parental love, a friendship love, and a God kind of love.

Jesus asks Peter if he loves Jesus with a God kind of love.

Peter responds that he loves Jesus with a friendship kind of love.

Jesus asks Peter again if he loves Jesus with a God kind of love.

Peter responds again that he loves Jesus with a friendship kind of love.

Jesus then asks Peter if he loves Jesus with a friendship kind of love.

Peter, again, tells Jesus that he loves him with a friendship kind of love.

Why the word games?

Remember *momentum*? Imagine the momentum of Peter. He's denied Jesus three times. How is he supposed to answer that he loves Jesus with a God kind of love when asked by Jesus?

He betrayed Jesus. He'd be a hypocrite if he said he loved him with a God kind of love. Peter is in the Dip and he's missed a big wave, with no more likely to come.

He feels as though he has failed.

So Jesus *goes* to Peter's level. Jesus asks Peter three times (the same number of times that Peter betrayed Jesus) if he loves him. Jesus lets Peter know that he's with him in the Dip, and that he's pulling him out of it. That stuff is over. It's behind us. What's done is done.

I know you don't think you love me with enough love, but it is. I know you love me. Waves are coming . . . let's work now and take this world to a better place. Let's change this world with love.

None of us have called down curses on someone who asked us if we knew the God that became a human after spending years following that human around. But even if we had, Jesus comes along with some break-fast and says "that's behind us. Do you love me *now* the best you can?"

There's more . . .

We're a people that generally like to determine life based on points. Points are arrivals or destinations. We like points because they make life really easy. We can set up a whole system of points and determine if people have arrived or not.

> Will they get to heaven?
> Have they reached the heaven point?

Can they enter my church?
Have they arrived at the church point?

Are they a Christian?
Have they crossed the Christian point?

Should I have a beer with them?
Are they worthy of the friendship point?

Can they babysit my kids?
Are they at a point where I can trust them like that?

At each point, we know if we're at a higher point; and if we are, we look down on the person at the lower point and look forward to bringing them up to where we are.

At each point, we know if we're at a lower point; and if we are, we look up to the person at the higher point and wonder if they can help us get to where they are.

The problem with points, beyond *constantly* judging people, is that we get very comfortable with our points—and where we're at. When we get to the point we think we've been trying to get to, we stop trying to move. We know it all. We've learned it all. We now understand God, the Bible, religion, pain, beauty, faith, and life. We honestly believe there's no need to learn anything else.

Many people are in this place: young and old, Christian and atheist, man and woman . . . it crosses and affects all categories of people and it might be the most dangerous place on Earth to be (and part of the reason that Solomon spends so much time trying to get us out of it). If you're below someone, you feel insufficient and if you're above them, you feel like you've got it all.

The good news is that there is another way and, I would argue, this is God's way.

Vectors.

Vectors are movements or trajectories or momentum.

When you look at the Bible with this in mind, it reads very differently and much more of it starts to make sense.

Frequently, Jesus encountered people who moved, or changed, positions (even it was just a little bit), including: a man lowered in through a roof, a paralytic, a Samaritan woman, a Roman centurion, a thief on a cross, and a tax collector.

The tax collector's name was Zaccheus, and he was up in a tree because he was short and couldn't see Jesus. Jesus told him to come down, and they ate dinner at Zaccheus' house. Zaccheus said he would give away half his possessions and four times the amount he cheated anyone out of.

Jesus said, "Salvation has come to this man's house."[160]

But Jesus told another man he needed to give away *all* his possessions.[161]

And Jesus told the Pharisees, who were seemingly much more religious than all of the "sinners," that they, in fact, were worse than the sinners.[162]

The story about the man who was lowered in through the roof says that Jesus saw the faith of *his friends* and, because of *that*, told the man that his sins were forgiven.[163]

And Jesus told a story about a son who was a mess and all he did was walk back home and he received a party while his older brother, who had been there all along, behaving, didn't get any party.[164]

What's the deal?

There are other stories of commanders of armies asking prophets of God if it's okay if they bow to other gods, and the prophet tells them to "go in peace."[165]

Go in peace?

It seems that God is all about vectors. Movement. Growth. Change. Evolution. The point, to God, is not whether you have arrived; the point is whether or not you are moving.

That's a fantastic thing. That means that even though it seems like we have so far to go, we can move somewhere today.

And it might mean something even better. We can even celebrate the movement that has occurred, no matter how small it is.

In each of those stories including the commander of armies, the tax collector, the Samaritan woman, the thief on the cross, and so on, there was movement, and God seems very pleased with movement because movement takes us places that points do not.

Points tend to get us stuck in Dips and formulas and idols. Vectors don't. And God, if nothing else, never wants to see humanity stuck. God is too busy trying to move us to beautiful, inspiring, and better places.

One of the biggest places we get stuck is shame. Brené Brown says that shame is "I am a mistake" and guilt is "I made a mistake." This is an incredibly important distinction because it means that shame is bad and guilt and regret are good. "Regret doesn't remind us that we did badly. It reminds us that we know we can do better."[166]

Shame will cement us to a point, which is why it is so deadly. Regret and guilt get us moving knowing there is somewhere to go.

The best way to fight shame is with empathy. Empathy says "me, too" and "I've been there" and "I know what you're going through."

Judgment is the worst thing for shame. It makes it grow.[167]

Judgment is everywhere in a point and formula world, which is why God gets so angry at people who throw their points and formulas in the faces of everyone "below" them. (This is a constant theme covered by Jesus in his discussion with the religious leaders of his day, and I believe it should be a constant theme among religious leaders today.)

Empathy is everywhere in a vector world. We're all trying to move, together. I have not finished moving and neither have you. Let's grow, let's change, let's keep going . . . together.

Rita Pierson tells a story of a student who was struggling in school. He took a test with 20 questions and got 18 of them wrong. Rita put a big plus two on the paper with a smiley face.

> He said, "Ms. Pierson, is this an F?"
>
> I said, "Yes."
>
> He said, "Then why'd you put a smiley face?"
>
> I said, "'Cause you on a roll. You got two right. You didn't miss them all." I said, "When we review this, won't you do better?"
>
> He said, "Yes, ma'am, I can do better."
>
> "You see, minus 18 sucks all the life out of you; plus two" I said, "ain't all bad."
>
> I don't know why we celebrate failure. Somewhere along the line, we started to think that if I point out to you what you don't do, or you didn't do, it will inspire you to do.
>
> That doesn't make sense to me. If I tell you what you've done right, it inspires you to do something else that's right. I want my students to always see the value of possibility, and that's what I wanted him to see. That I am worth more, I can do more, I am more. Plus two said that; minus 18 would not have said that.[168]

Ms. Pierson has transformed the educational trajectory of students by telling them they are worth *more* than points. She celebrates movement more than arrivals, because arrivals will never happen if we don't start moving.

We are not called to move down to others, just as we are not called to get others to the spot where we are. What we are called to do is walk with everyone *somewhere*. We are called to be moving and no matter where we are, the point is to move deeper into the pool, higher up the mountain, and further into the love of God.

Which leads us to the final point.

I tend to spend a lot of time thinking about *them*.

> The church I read about on a blog.

> The guy on Facebook who makes those posts.

> The girl who has that blog.

> That group and the way they treat people.

> That other group and the way they spend money.

> That other group and the way they spend money and treat people and do it all in the name of God.

I don't know about you, but sometimes I'm even consumed with them.

> I can't believe *they* said that.

> I can't believe *he* bought that.

> I can't believe *she* did that.

> I can't believe *they* built that.

> I can't believe *they* wrote that.

Then sometimes I talk to God about *them*.

I complain that things aren't going the way I think they should be going. Especially when *those* people are doing *those* things and ruining my reputation, hurting people, etc.

At the end of that breakfast story with Jesus, Peter, and the disciples, Jesus tells Peter that life is going to get hard. He tells Peter that despite all his mistakes, he has faith in Peter to do amazing things for love and for Jesus, but that's it going to be difficult. In fact, Peter may even have to follow through on that promise he made; he may have to eventually die for Jesus and for the love that he brought.

After he tells Peter this, Peter asks Jesus what will happen to another disciple. (Just like I often do: "What about *him*?")

Jesus responds with a great answer: "What is that to you? You must follow me."

God, have you seen what they are doing in Your name? It's horrible.

> "What is that to you?"

God, have you seen what he is doing to people over there? It's tragic.

> "What is that to you?"

God, have you heard what that person said about you? And *they* claim to be a Christian?

> "What is that to you?"

> *You* follow me.

It fights everything inside of our ego. It beats on the walls of our pride, half-tortured by the thought of it, that it might be *us*. *We* might be the ones who need to hear the message. *We* might be the ones who need to move, to change, to adjust. *We* might be the ones who are wrong.

We can hardly stand to say it, especially in religious settings. And so we always turn the spotlight away from us and toward them. Even better, we turn it toward something that we don't even struggle with or would never struggle with. The less the temptation, the more focused we become; the more the temptation, the more silent we become. The ego no longer fights, but relaxes into a happy, almost drug-addicted state. Once we can focus on them and their mistakes, our own mistakes fade away.

Stop. No more. This message is for *you*. It always has been and it always will be. If you heard it, ingest it, immerse yourself in it, and remember the constant words of Jesus.

You. Follow me.

Them? What's it to you?

I got to hang out with Rob Bell and 49 others for two days in Laguna Beach. It was an amazing time. We surfed and ate good food and talked about lots of things. One of the great things Rob said while we were there is: "What they are doing is not interesting," in reference to this passage.

Ever since I heard it, I loved it. I've tried to make it define me. I've tried to bring it into conversations, I've tried to live it.

It's amazing when you are aware of it, how often our conversations end up being about someone else or some other group and what they are doing. It's amazing how fast, and politely, you can kill those conversations by saying, "I really don't find it all that interesting. What about you?"

It's amazing how once you say that a few times, and get your family and friends saying it, that it becomes true.

They really aren't that interesting because we don't control them in any way, shape, or form. The only thing *they* are really good at is distracting us from what we are supposed to be doing. The only thing *they* are really good at is distracting us from living; they make us less alive.

We have two very scary tendencies as humans: one is to seek out information that confirms information we already think we know; and second is to hang out with people that have those same beliefs that we think we know. As we continue to hang out with people who only confirm our beliefs, our beliefs become more extreme and everyone else becomes more extremely wrong.

We end up with virtual "clubs" and virtual "memberships" made of people who are fairly certain they know everything and everyone else doesn't. Of course, those people happen to agree with us on what we know and what everyone else doesn't know. Once we find ourselves in some of these groups, we tend to think that we have it all figured out and that everyone else doesn't.

We all worship an idol together.

We become obsessed with *those* people. Everything we see or hear is ammo to prove them wrong and prove us right and never the other way around.

I would encourage you to simply not go there.

What's it to you?

They are not interesting.

What *is* interesting, however, and it's probably one of the biggest reasons I still call myself a Christian, is the question:

Who are *you*?

To summarize the mystics, if that's possible, I think they would say that the most important question one can ask is: Who am I?

The reason they say this is because we run from this question in every form and in every stage. Instead of asking that question, which is a complicated and deep question, we dive into the formulas and boats and idols just like Solomon has been saying.

Even though we know *they* never work.

What do I need to do to be a better parent?

Who are you? Your kids will be far more impressed by who you are than by what you do.

What do I need to do to be a better partner?

Who are you? The relationship will go up or down based on that.[169]

What do I need to believe in or do to follow God?

Who are you? Does God really care what you mentally acknowledge or physically do just because you're supposed to do it to get something?

What do I need to do to avoid . . . or get . . . or find . . . or achieve . . . or make sure of . . . or . . . We are desperate to learn how this life works. So we are always asking what caused *this* to happen to *him* and what caused *that* to happen to *her*. We are always trying to learn the formula that we can just plug in and make it work for us. To figure it out. And we come up with laws and rules and guidelines and prayers and theologies and facts and whatever we can to make sure we don't have to address the only question that really matters which is:

Who are you?

But that's so hard. That takes patience and introspection and effort to answer and address.

Let me tell you how I believe Christianity answers this question, and why I'm a big fan (and follower).

> Who am I?
>
> I am a beautiful creature created by a mysterious, but good God. I'm loved and always with this God. I'm pulled along by this God to rise above pain, fears, formulas, images, and idols and led to bask in the awe and wonder of everything around me. This God helps me rise out of whatever Dip I'm in and leads me to create something beautiful and mysterious and original for myself, and others, until they recognize who they really are and how much this God loves us and wants us to love each other.

One step at a time.

> Love liked a child.[170]

> Perfectly righteous.[171]

Free from any kind of condemnation.[172]

Blameless.[173]

Inseparable from the love of God.[174]

A precious, beautiful work of art.[175]

Filled with the peace and joy of God.[176]

And on and on the story goes when it talks about *me*. If I just believe it. Accept it. Take it and run with it to greener pastures, bigger parties, and more colorful, vibrant lives where the black and white and charts and formulas and rules and laws become less necessary because we are different at our core.

When the world becomes *that* colorful and the pastures that big, the beauty and good occupies us to such a degree that we don't have any time to notice *them* and what *they* are doing.[177]

Life gets too big for the little things.

What are *you* going to do today to ease pain, experience life, soak in mystery, gaze at *whoa*, to love, and to rise?

Just a little more.

How are *you* going to be free?

A tiny step more.

Where are the waves?

How are *you* going to make this island called *life* a better one for us all?

Just a touch more.

Remember: everything breathes. There is life everywhere, just waiting for you to stop and appreciate it *as* God, and *with* God.

How are *you* going to live?

Breathe?
Experience?
Move?
Create?
Evolve?

Just a little more.

You are worth it. You have value. You can do more, and you have a God on your side who will take you there.

Give, create, love, move others. Change the world as you are changed.

Today. Right now.

As

you

finish

these

words,

let's begin.

seventeen

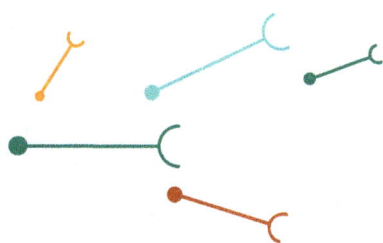

gazelles.

This is an epilogue of sorts. Or maybe it's more of an exercise or meditation. Some people aren't big fans of any of those, but I would encourage you to give it a try.

You can always just read through it first and see what you think.

You can also do it more than once.

To get things going, grab your MP3 player, a stereo, a computer, or some kind of music-playing device to play a song on. And then do whatever you need to do for the song to be loud. Turn up the volume, put on some headphones . . . do what you've got to do.

The louder, the better.

I know this sounds a little weird, but there is a plan here.

After you've got your system ready to go, you'll need a song. This will need to be a song that moves, relaxes, inspires, or just speaks to you. Maybe it's *Fix You* by Coldplay or maybe it's a classic Johnny Cash tune. And if you can't think of anything, then I strongly recommend listening to a song by M83.

Intro or *Steve McQueen* will work perfectly.[178]

Get the song ready and get *yourself* ready. If you can go outside, even better. On a deck, on a beach, on a park bench, on a chair in your front yard, wherever! It's not a requirement, but it will work better.

This is not emotional manipulation; this is emotional saturation, and it's good and right and healthy, but it won't work unless you are ready and open to it.

Once you are ready, stop.

As you're reading this, think of all the things you have to do and all the stresses in your life—the anxiety and the worry.

And, now, don't worry about them. Let go of them. Give up the control, give up the stress, and

let . . . it . . . go.

> The bathroom will eventually get cleaned.

> The kids will get to their game.

> The job will get done.

> The paper will get written.

> The project will launch.

Stop. Rest.

Breathe. Relax.

It's okay.

You are going to close your eyes until all of those things that you have to do are gone, and when they are, open up your eyes again.

Now, play that song. Listen to it for a moment. But really listen. Pay attention to the voices, instruments, and the words like you never have before.

Just breathe for a moment.

Start thinking of those fears. You know the ones. The trolls. They haunt you in your sleep and they mock you in the car, at your job, on your runs, at the doctor's office, at school, or wherever they get a chance.

And you are so sick of them—sick of their taunting and their reminders.

They control you way more than you want them to and you despise them for it.

Maybe they're about:

money
or sickness
or success
or marriage
or kids,
or loneliness,
or addiction
or the future
or the possibility of losing any of the things listed above.

Here are some of my fears that may trigger some in you:

The fear of losing my edge.
The fear of not being enough (shame).
The fear of not being able to connect to people anymore.
The fear of my job getting boring.
The fear of telling people the wrong thing.
The fear of losing the great things I have.

If you don't think you have them, you're not thinking hard enough. We all have them. Give them some time to come up again.

Write them on a piece of paper or just jot them down in your head.

I like to imagine a stack of tiles with each one holding my fear written in black Sharpie.

Now, start smashing those tiles. Maybe with a big hammer. If they are on a piece of paper, imagine them bursting into flames. Or, imagine throwing them into a fire.

Whatever they are written on, destroy it. If you need to swear, do it. If you need to say "F--- you" to each one of them out loud, do it. If there are people around you, they might think you're crazy, but let's be honest, there are worse things than swearing . . . like being controlled by fear.

Remember: Those fears are nothing to be afraid of anymore, and there isn't a place where pain does not exist, so what's the use in dreading it?

No matter what, God is there.

With the fears. Always.
With the hurt. Always.
With the oppressed. Always.

The desires.

They are next. They are so closely intertwined with the fears that we barely recognize them most of the time.

But start thinking about them.

Maybe they are about money
or health
or success
or kids
or loneliness
or addiction
or the future
or the possibility of getting any of the things listed above.

Here are some of my desires that may trigger some in you:

The desire to be accepted more, heard by more people, and yet, stay who I am and be authentic.
The desire to not have to worry about money anymore.
The desire to see more of the world.
The desire for my kids to be strong and humble, convincing and athentic, and to know who they are.

All of them are within the same category of thought, though . . .

For *this* to happen and *that* to go this way and if . . . then . . .

Now, do the same thing to your desires that you did to your fears. Write them on something and smash them to pieces. Burn them. One at a time. Watch the embers glow or the pieces of tile explode into the air.

Because they may come true, or they may not, but if they are what life is about, then that's just not . . .

living.

Now, with those things out of the way, look around you. Start to experience the colors of life. You have to really look to see it.

Look at pine needles, at leaves on a tree, at blades of grass, at your partner sleeping beside you, at your kids, at the blue sky, at the beach, at the subway windows, at the cars driving by, at the people drinking coffee, at the people laughing. I don't know where you are, but look at it in all of its ordinary, sacred detail.

Smell   it.
The humidity. The air conditioning. The salt water. The candles. The rain. I don't know where you're at, but really smell it.

Feel   it.
Feel the air coming into your nostrils. The hot air on your lips. Taste the salt of your skin. Cold? Feel it. Hot? Feel it.

Feel the pages of the book or the device you're holding. Notice your calluses or the lack of them on your skin. Feel your heart beating and your lungs functioning. Feel your socks or the sheets or the carpet or the wood floor.

Start letting go of all the things you are holding on to. Let go of the false images of God that you keep clinging to, like a golden cow. Let go of your insistence on knowing everything about that God or the way the world functions.

Start thinking about love and God's love for you.
And your love for others.
And their love for you.
And people who have no love and need love.

Tell God you want to live. Right now.

Not then. Not someday.

This is living.

This is life.

Say the words out loud. This is life. I mean it really is. Honestly, what about this current moment is not living?

What are you waiting for?

No, really, what are you waiting for?

For me, this all happened on a Friday when the kids were out of school and I was running in the woods.

There I was. Thinking about all of this.

Running is a stopping experience for me. It's like no other. When I'm running, my brain is free to think unlike any other time in my life. So I was already stopped.

And then I started going through the easy stuff. I don't need a lot of money, but sometimes I want a lot of money. I make myself feel better because I tell myself that I only want money to travel, as though that is some kind of noble dream. I don't want money to buy cars, I want money to travel to New Zealand, Iceland, Sweden, Costa Rica, and Bora Bora. I get mad watching *The Amazing Race* because I keep saying to my family, "I should have been on this season."

My family gets mad at me for being too loud.

I know God looks down on me, so proud, and says, "Wow, Ryan, you are amazing. No one wants money for *that*."

Then I started going through my fears.

I listed them off.

Which led me to my desires.

I listed them off.

The song *Intro* by M83 had been on my iPod, but I really just *heard* it for the first time. I had, of course, listened to it before, but I started to hear it in an all-new way. It was louder and in my face and moving and inspiring.

Time and chance, maybe.

When M83 reaches my ear like *that*, my soul smiles.

And then something happened.

Everything changed.

I looked up. I think I had been looking up, but I looked up and saw things I didn't normally see. It was surreal.

Pine needles with drops of dew resting on their tips. I saw each translucent little bubble as I passed by it.

Gray skies, that I had been mad at earlier, were suddenly beautiful in the way they made the colors below them pop.

Snow was melting on the path, and dirt and leaves and green were beginning to appear beneath them.

I saw the details of the bark on the trees.

And then I felt. I felt my sweat dripping on my forehead. I felt the calluses on my fingers and I felt the heat emanating from my skin. I felt my feet hit the soft ground of the trail.

I smelled the air. The cool, clean, crisp air with hints of pine and dirt and life.

I found myself running what felt like faster than I had ever run in my life—like a gazelle. Was I in a movie? The song was building and I was seeing everything, and I was flying through the woods, leaping over logs, jumping over branches, skipping and gliding across the ground as though I were some kind of superman.

The trees became a blur, and I looked up at the sky and said out loud, "God, what am I waiting for? This is life. Right here. Right now. It doesn't get any better than this."

And my tears flowed like a waterfall, streaming down my cheeks and to the ground. I kept running and I kept soaking in every moment and I kept telling God: "I want *this* all the time."

Just telling this story almost gets me crying again.

I was alive.

I was a sobbing, fast, happy, energized gazelle who was alive.

I wasn't riding a bike trail,
owning a car wash,
or running like those caribou . . .

just to survive.

I was running like a gazelle . . .

to live.

Extraordinary life. And it's always there for us, every ordinary moment.

That is success. That is heaven.

Fear God. Soak in the mystery. Love. Rise.

Let's go change the world.

This is breathing in the way we are supposed to breathe, and I hope we may all be able to find it in every time, in every place, and in everything.

eighteen

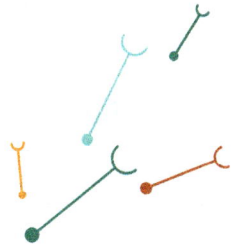

nothing new.

Solomon writes that there is nothing new under the sun and I certainly don't claim to have come up with anything new here. I do, however, hope that my language, perspective, and story have helped to reveal old ideas in new ways . . . in the way that others have done the same for me.

Below is a list of authors and speakers whom I've let my soul soak in as much as possible. If you liked this book, at all, Google them today. You'll find speeches, videos, podcasts, books, and you won't be disappointed. I am who I am because of them, and this book is what it is because of *their* language, perspective, and stories that have impacted *me* in monstrous ways. They are my biggest influences.

Jesus

(and then alphabetical order)

Rob Bell
Brené Brown
Jacques Ellul
Seth Godin
Anthony de Mello
Tony Jones
Thomas Merton
Steven Pressfield
Richard Rohr
Peter Rollins

Endnotes are not always the most exciting part of a book, but I'd encourage you to skim through them. You'll find some treats, as well as other authors and works that have, obviously, had a direct impact on me and this work.

caribou.

1 Rob Fairbanks was the pastor of the church. We went out to lunch one day, and he said I should plant a church. I've thanked Rob many times and I will continue to do so. He saw something in me or heard something from God—maybe both—but whatever it was, I'm very grateful.

2 If you were to receive only one daily email, it should be this one. Richard Rohr, "Resurrection as the Revelation of What Was Always True," http://myemail.constantcontact.com/Daily-Meditation-- Resurrection-as-the-Revelation-of-What-Was-Always-True----Frame----May-4--2013.html?soid=1103098668616&aid=ubFPszTNpfc, May 3, 2013.

yacine.

3 This podcast is worth listening to. I loved Macklemore even more after listening to it than I did before, and respected him a ton for his honesty and outlook on life. "Macklemore," Nerdist Podcast, http://www.nerdist.com/2013/03/nerdist-podcast-macklemore/.

4 I actually found this quote after the book was just about done. It's a good one. Tom Wolfe, quoted in Robert Short, *A Time to Be Born—A Time to Die* (New York: Harper and Row, 1973), IX.

5 The story is in 1 Kings 3.

islands.

6 Matthew 7.

7 The story is long and goes from Exodus 19-32. While some might disagree and say that the people were fashioning images of other "gods," in Exodus 32:4, Aaron says "This is your Elohim who brought you out of Egypt." Gen. 1:1 says "Elohim created the Earth." In Gen. 32:5, Aaron says "tomorrow will be a feast for Jehovah"—another name attributed to the "one true God." The people who made the cow don't seem confused as to what the cow is supposed to represent.

8 Ecclesiastes 7:14.

9 Ecclesiastes 11:7-8.

10 Schwartz says it all, and even though it's a little old at this point (is 2004 old?), it's still worth reading. Schwartz also has some great TED Talks—check them out. Barry Schwartz, *The Paradox of Choice: Why More is Less* (New York: HarperCollins, 2004), 106.

11 I'll be quoting Agassi's autobiography quite a bit, and for good reason. It's not only the best autobiography I've ever read—it's one of the best books I've ever read. If you don't like tennis, it doesn't matter; it's an exquisite read. It's also like reading a modern day version of Ecclesiastes. Andre Agassi, *Open: An Autobiography* (Vintage, 2009), Kindle edition, 160.

12 Ibid., 232.

13 Ibid.

14 Ibid., 250.

15 Anthony de Mello is my hero. He offers unbelievably amazing stuff all the time. Read anything of his—anything!—you won't be disappointed. Anthony de Mello, *Awakening: Conversations with the Masters* (Image, 2009), Kindle edition, 130.

pain.

16 Associated Press, "Plane Kills Beach Jogger in Emergency Landing," News.Yahoo.com, March 16, 2010, http://www.nbcnews.com/id/35896336/ns/us_news-life/t/plane-kills-beach-jogger-emergency-landing/#.UgA7P5LCaM4. A truly tragic story of time and chance.

17 Gautam Naik and Alan Cullision, "The Search is on for Meteorite," *The Wall Street Journal*, February 19, 2013, http://online.wsj.com/article/SB10001424127887323764804578312264130040432.html. There are all kinds of facts, numbers, and estimates on meteors.

18 This article came out while I was editing, and I had to add it. John Johnson, "Russian Meteor's Shock Wave Circled the Earth—Twice," *USA Today*, June 29, 2013, http://www.usatoday.com/story/tech/2013/06/29/newser-russia-meteor/2475293/.

19 More facts, numbers, and estimates on meteors. Phil Black and Laura Smith-Spark, "Russia Starts Cleanup After Meteor Strike," CNN.com, February 19, 2013, http://www.cnn.com/2013/02/16/world/europe/russia-meteor-shower.

20 I heard about this during Lent from a student who goes to our church. Heartbreaking. Alexa Vaughn, "Maple Valley woman among the dead in crash at Vegas shooting scene," *The Seattle Times*, February 22, 2013, http://blogs.seattletimes.com/today/2013/02/maple-valley-woman-among-the-dead-in-crash-at-vegas-shooting-scene/.

21 Greg Boyd is incredibly smart and pretty funny as well. And he has some thoughts about the "blueprint" worldview that you should know. Gregory A. Boyd. Is God to Blame? *Moving Beyond Pat Answers to the Problem of Suffering* (IVP Books, 2003), Kindle edition, 58.

22 Speaking of Greg Boyd, he's one of the biggest voices of what is called Open Theism. Worth looking into. You can start by just googling it. You'll find a plethora of information and disagreement. Between you and me, I'm a pretty big fan of it.

23 A way too broad summary, but this is what most of Leviticus says.

24 Ecclesiastes 9:1-6.

25 Ecclesiastes 9:3.

26 Ecclesiastes 9:3-6.

27 Ecclesiastes 9:11-12.

28 Ecclesiastes 3:1-7.

29 The story behind Geoff (who was injured) Carlos (the man who helped save his life) is unbelievable. And from what I understand, Geoff immediately awoke from his surgery and said, "Give me a pad and paper; I know what the guy looks like." Wow. Bridget Murphy, "My son was just in the wrong place at the wrong time," Associated Press, April 16, 2013, http://www.katu.com/news/national/Boston-tragedy-hits-even-harder-as-victims-lives-come-to-light-203311721.html.

30 Alain de Botton is a gentleman and a scholar and someone I would love to have a beer, wine, or a cup of tea with. Atheists who don't act like fundamentalists are some of my favorite people, and I think de Botton would be as well. "Alain de Botton: A kinder, gentler philosophy of success." Filmed July 2009. TED video. Posted July 2009. http://www.ted.com/talks/alain_de_botton_a_kinder_gentler_philosophy_of_success.html.

life.

31 ibid.

32 Agassi, *Open*, 348.

33 de Mello, *Awakening*, 128.

back to pain.

34 Agassi, *Open*, 178.

35 A friend of mine told me about this book, but I haven't read it yet. I need to, though. Michael J. Fox, *Lucky Man: A Memoir* (New York: Hyperion, 2002), 6.

36 If you have never read a book and cried, I challenge you to read this and not shed tears. It's beautifully moving, tragic, and so good to read. Sheldon Vanauken, *A Severe Mercy* (New York: Harper Row, 1987), 18.

37 It may be one of those books you read in high school and didn't get. Read it again; it's so good. Aldous Huxley, *Brave New World* (RosettaBooks, 2010), Kindle edition. 3085.

38 "What Runs Through Your Mind As Your Plane Is Crashing?" NPR TED Radio Hour, June 28, 2013, http://www.npr.org/templates/transcript/transcript.php?storyId=195233144.

39 Ecclesiastes 7:2-4.

mystery.

40 Ecclesiastes 11:5.

41 We actually haven't known until fairly recently what causes wind. No wonder it was worshiped. This article is one of many that "explains" it. Jerry Coffey, "What Causes Wind," Universe Today, December 10, 2010, http://www.universetoday.com/82329/what-causes-wind/#ixzz2X-pv7zMFQ.

42 I just went to Wikipedia to look up human fertilization. I would have referenced an encyclopedia, but who uses those anymore? Also, if you've never donated to Wikipedia, you should look into how they operate. You'll probably donate after doing so. "Human fertilization," *Wikipedia*, http://en.wikipedia.org/wiki/Human_fertilization.

43 This is another TED Talk introduced to me through NPR's TED Radio Hour. Pretty amazing stuff here. "Alexander Tsiaras: Conception to birth – visualized." Filmed December 2010. TED video. Posted November 2011. http://www.ted.com/talks/alexander_tsiaras_conception_to_birth_visualized.html.

44 John 3. Jesus talks to Nicodemus about the Kingdom of God in this often quoted, and very mysterious, chapter.

45 If you don't know what any of these are, count yourself lucky. If you do, well, I hope you saw a tract because your Sunday school teacher had one and not because a stranger gave you one on a sidewalk or in a restaurant somewhere. And if you ever wore one of those "salvation bracelets" with the five colored beads on them that were meant to represent "the gospel," well . . . I did, too. My only problem was that I told the only person to ever ask me about the bracelet, and if the colors meant anything, that it was just a fashion thing. I felt guilty until I realized that Jesus didn't wear salvation bracelets either.

46 This quote actually came from a book that had nothing to do with science, but about why things catch on and are contagious. It turns out that the things that create wonder and awe catch on. I wonder if the reason Christianity has lost so much of its appeal is because we took all the wonder out of it by answering all of the questions? Ironic. Jonah Berger, *Contagious: Why Things Catch On* (Simon & Schuster, 2013), Kindle edition, 102.

47 I don't claim to have a handle on the world of quantum physics, but it appears to be complicated, magical, and mysterious for those who

do. And for me. For a good introduction, check out this biography on one of the most famous names in quantum physics. John Gribbin, *Erwin Schrodinger and the Quantum Revolution* (Wiley, 2013), Kindle edition.

48 Ibid. Kindle Locations 2156-2158.

49 Ecclesiastes 11.1-4.

50 Ecclesiastes 8:17.

51 John 6.

52 You can read all about awe enhancing people's perception of time right here. Melanie Rudd, Kathleen D. Vohs, and Jennifer Aaker, "Awe Expands People's Perception of Time, Alters Decision Making, and Enhances Well-Being," Stanford.edu, http://faculty-gsb.stanford.edu/aaker/pages/documents/TimeandAwe2012_workingpaper.pdf.

53 I would call The Dish a blog, but it's so much bigger and better than that. It's a news source, and I highly recommend it to anyone. The Dish has led me to so many articles I reference in this book that I had to give it credit here. Andrew Sullivan, "Wonder Through The Ages," The Dish (blog), July 3, 2013, http://dish.andrewsullivan.com/2013/07/03/wonder-through-the-ages/; Jesse Prinz, "How Wonder Works," *Aeon Magazine*, June 12, 2013, http://www.aeonmagazine.com/oceanic-feeling/why-wonder-is-the-most-human-of-all-emotions/.

54 The Hebrew creation poem says that the fruit was good for "wisdom" and that the woman was tempted by the snake who talked about the knowledge of "good and evil" that the fruit offered. This whole desire to know, in the story of Genesis 3, at least, got us into trouble.

55 This is a classic book from a classic thinker. G.K. Chesterton, *Orthodoxy*, (Simon & Brown, 2012), 14.

stop.

56 If you haven't heard of Brené Brown, you might be living under a rock. She's an amazing woman. Her TED Talks are monsters, and her books are smart and eye-opening. Everything she has talked about on shame, guilt, and vulnerability has stuck with me, and I use it constantly.

Brené Brown, *Daring Greatly: How the Courage to Be Vulnerable Transforms the Way We Live, Love, Parent, and Lead* (Gotham, 2012), Kindle edition, 137.

57 Genesis 1 and 2.

58 Brené Brown rocks some of these themes in her second and famous TED Talk. "Brené Brown: Listening to shame." Filmed March 2012. TED video. Posted March 2012. http://www.ted.com/talks/brene_brown_listening_to_shame.html.

let god go.

59 Barry McDonald, Philip Zaleski, and Satish Kumar, *Seeing God Everywhere: Essays on Nature and the Sacred* (*Perennial Philosophy*) (Bloomington, IN: World Wisdom, Inc., 2003), 59.

60 I first heard all of this in a series of *Awareness* recordings. Then a friend gave me this to read, which was great, but I still listen to the recordings every chance I get. I've heard it more times than I can count. And it always pops up, from time to time, on a run or in the car. St. Thomas also said, "About God, we cannot say what He is but rather what He is not. And so we cannot speak about how He is but rather

how He is not." Anthony De Mello, *Awareness* (New York, NY: Doubleday, 1992), 47.

61 Greg Mariotti, "Day & Night: The Quote," Pixar Talk (blog), http://www.pixartalk.com/2010/06/day-night-the-quote/. Day & Night is probably my favorite Pixar short film. Although the quote is attributed to Dr. Wayne Deyer (from a 1970's lecture), it sounds similar to a speech given by Einstein.

let the trolls go.

62 This book blew my mind the first time I read it. You will never look at terrorism, cancer, or ads for alarm systems the same way. And that's a good thing. We need less fear in our lives. Daniel Gardner, *The Science of Fear: How the Culture of Fear Manipulates Your Brain* (Penguin Group, 2008), Kindle edition, 288.

63 I've been meeting with two Jesuit priests and have come to realize that so many of the "new," progressive thoughts in the Protestant world have been in the Jesuit world for generations. Sorry, guys, we're slow like that sometimes. This book summarizes Jesuit thinking in a fun, educational way. James Martin, *The Jesuit Guide to (Almost) Everything: A Spirituality for Real Life* (HarperCollins, 2010), Kindle edition. 671.

64 Ecclesiastes 7:2-4.

65 Martin, *The Jesuit Guide*, 671.

66 The stories of Jesus telling people not to be afraid fill the gospels. Luke 8 and Mark 4 become a sequence of 3 stories all about fear. When Mary and Zecharias are told of the coming birth of Jesus and John the Baptist, both are also told to not be afraid.

67 de Mello, *Awakening: Conversations with the Masters*, 122.

68 Matthew 5.

69 Ecclesiastes 3.12-13.

70 Ecclesiastes 3:22.

71 Ecclesiastes 5:18-20.

72 Ecclesiastes 7:10.

73 Ecclesiastes 11:9.

74 Ecclesiastes 11:10.

75 Ecclesiastes 7:24-25.

76 Ecclesiastes 8:15.

77 Ecclesiastes 9:7-10.

78 Brené talks about this in terms of joy. Brown, *Daring Greatly*, 125.

79 I had the pleasure of having lunch and beer with Peter Rollins and asked him to explain all of his wild ways of looking at the world. Read at least one of his books if you haven't already. This one talks a good bit about idols and might be a good place to start. Peter Rollins, *The Idolatry of God: Breaking Our Addiction to Certainty and Satisfaction* (Simon & Schuster, Inc., 2013), Kindle edition.

80 de Mello, *Awareness*, 76.

81 For more on these ideas which are very much Ignatian Spirituality, check out Martin, *The Jesuit Guide*.

fear god.

82 Ecclesiastes 5:7.

83 Genesis 20. (for the most part).

84 Ezekiel 16:49-50. It's really irritating that people continue to point to Sodom and Gomorrah as some kind of illustration of anything to do with homosexuality. Not that I don't understand it. While most of us aren't homosexuals, just about every one of us living in America today is guilty of what those cities *were* destroyed for.

85 Luke 1.

86 Luke 1:74-75.

87 Luke 12:4-7.

88 Mark 11:18.

89 Acts 13:50.

90 Acts 17:4.

91 Acts 13:26.

92 Acts 2:5.

93 Acts 10:2.

94 Romans 8:15.

95 2 Corinthians 5:11.

96 Philippians 2:12.

97 1 John 4:16-18.

98 Revelation 15:4.

99 Anthony de Mello talks about this idea, and I dove into it one Sunday in church. We had someone taste a cookie, look at a photo, and listen to a song, and then write about it in Spanish. Another person translated the Spanish and we read it aloud. Guess how many people got what was translated into English? Right. And that's what we do with the Bible so often.

100 Judges 13.

101 Matthew 21:15.

102 I really don't know where I'd be with this whole "Christian thing" if it weren't for Rob Bell and his books and speaking. His latest book (as of this writing) is a good one filled with similar thoughts and ideas to this one. Rob Bell, *What We Talk About When We Talk About God* (Harper-Collins, 2013), Kindle edition.

103 Ecclesiastes 3:14.

104 Of course de Mello has a story that sums this up beautifully. de Mello, *Awakening: Conversations with the Masters*, 186.

105 This is a fun video. Andrew Liszewski, "Just How Incomprehensibly Massive Is the Universe? (Hint: Even Bigger Than That)," Gizmodo.com, February 25, 2013, http://gizmodo.com/5986798/just-how-incompre-hensibly-massive-is-the-universe-hint-even-bigger-than-that.

106 "Are We Alone In The Universe?" NPR TED Radio Hour, February 13, 2013, http://www.npr.org/templates/transcript/transcript.php?storyId=172140077

107 "How Did A Mistake Unlock One Of Space's Mysteries?" NPR TED Radio Hour, February 15, 2013, http://www.npr.org/templates/transcript/transcript.php?storyId=172139216

108 This is an incredibly interesting article. Raymond Tallis, "Philosophy isn't dead yet," The Guardian, May 26, 2013, http://www.guardian.co.uk/commentisfree/2013/may/27/physics-philosophy-quantum-relativity-einstein.

109 Astronomy Picture of the Day August 4, 2012. http://apod.nasa.gov/apod/ap120804.html

110 "Alain de Botton: A kinder, gentler philosophy of success." Filmed July 2009. TED video. Posted July 2009. http://www.ted.com/talks/alain_de_botton_a_kinder_gentler_philosophy_of_success.html

111 If you haven't heard or read this speech, you need to. Today. It's available in a book form. David Foster Wallace, *This Is Water: Some Thoughts, Delivered on a Significant Occasion, About Living a Compassionate Life* (Little, Brown and Company, 2009); and also in a great article: "Plain old untrendy troubles and emotions," The Guardian, September 19, 2008, http://www.guardian.co.uk/books/2008/sep/20/fiction or a video (although it has been removed in the past) available here: http://vimeo.com/66775750

112 Ecclesiastes 7:16-18.

love.

113 Matthew 22:36-40.

114 John 13:34.

115 Colossians 3:12-14.

116 Romans 13:10.

117 Luke 10:25-37.

118 Romans 13:10.

119 Matthew 5:34-38.

120 Matthew 5:34-38.

121 Ibid.

122 Galatians 5:22.

123 Hebrews 19:24.

124 1 John 14:16-20.

125 1 John 4:7-8.

126 1 Corinthians 13. All of the "love is" lines come from the chapter.

127 Translated by George Fyler Townsend. *Aesop's Fables* (p. 67). Amazon Digital Services, Inc..

128 C.S. Lewis says something similar about true humility in *Mere Christianity.*

129 Agassi, *Open*, 254.

130 Wallace, "Plain old untrendy troubles and emotions."

131 Rollins, *The Idolatry of God*, 144.

132 This quote is everywhere, and it's hard to find the original source so I'm just referencing one place I found it. I don't own the book where Nouwen wrote this, but I do own others. You should as well. Brad Brisco, "Missional and Henri Nouwen," Missional Church Network, March 20, 2007, http://missionalchurchnetwork.com/missional-and-henri-nouwen/.

133 1 Corinthians 13:1-3.

134 If you want a book that carries this idea further and will probably rock your world, check this one out. It's old and some of the language is tough but we don't even know who wrote it. How cool is that? And it's concepts are pretty amazing if you can get beyond some of the

language. It's all about *not* knowing God. William Johnston, *The Cloud of Unknowing: and The Book of Privy Counseling* (The Doubleday Religious Publishing Group, 2012), Kindle edition.

just be human.

135 This story is taken from John 14.

136 I spent two days with Rob Bell and 50 other people in Laguna Beach, where he said this. He's made the remark in other interviews as well and strikes some of these themes in Rob Bell, *Velvet Elvis: Repainting the Christian Faith* (HarperOne, 2012), Kindle edition. as well.

137 I watched this documentary with my kids. Besides seeing all the great rappers from my youth, I heard the f-word and n-word about 80,000 times, so be warned. *Something from Nothing: The Art of Rap*, Indomina, September 2012.

138 More elaboration on this idea can be found here: Richard Rohr, *Things Hidden: Scripture as Spirituality* (Cincinnati, OH: St. Anthony Messenger Press, 2008), 17.

139 There is a ton of disagreement among theologians and translators as to the gender of the Holy Spirit. In Hebrew and Greek, it's most often feminine. This passage translates as "he," but there are theologians who would disagree and say it should be feminine, including Daniel Wallace from Dallas Theological Seminary. If there is disagreement, I'm going with feminine because it reminds me that God is bigger than I think. There's also something comforting about a feminine deity at times. Daniel B. Wallace, *Greek Grammar Beyond the Basics: An Exegetical Syntax of the New Testament* (Grand Rapids: Zondervan, 1996), 332.

140 John 5.

141 If you do anything creative—ever—you have to read this book. You just have to. I've read it too many times to count. Steven Pressfield, *The War of Art: Break Through the Blocks and Win Your Inner Creative Battles* (New York, NY: Black Irish Entertainment, LLC, 2002), 165.

rise.

142 "William Kamkwamba: How I built a windmill." Filmed June 2007. TED video. Posted July 2007. http://www.ted.com/talks/william_kamkwamba_on_building_a_windmill.html; Faith Karimi, "Malawian boy uses wind to power hope, electrify village," CNN.com, October 5, 2009, http://edition.cnn.com/2009/WORLD/africa/10/05/malawi.wind.boy/. William's story is amazing, and his TED Talk is fantastic.

143 Phil Richards, "How a $10 bill changed a Colts rookie's life," USA Today, December 28, 2012. http://www.usatoday.com/story/sports/nfl/colts/2012/12/28/indianapolis-colts-dwayne-allen-changed-his-life-with-a-ten-dollar-bill/1797141/. Dwayne's story is a great one.

144 You'll definitely fall in love, and maybe cry, if you watch this video. Tyler Bastian, *Everything is Incredible, Film About a Disabled Honduran Man Who Has Been Building a Homemade Helicopter*, Vimeo.com, http://vimeo.com/35545694.

145 Ibid.

146 Seth Godin, *The Dip: A Little Book That Teaches You When to Quit (and When to Stick)* (Portfolio, 2007), Kindle edition, 17.

147 Ibid., 19.

148 "Are Some Things Universally Beautiful?" NPR TED Radio Hour, March 19, 2013, http://www.npr.org/templates/transcript/transcript.php?storyId=174726813.

149 Godin, *The Dip*, 52.

150 You will laugh out loud with this book. It's hilarious, and then it stabs you with truth. Good good stuff. Tripp York, *The Devil Wears Nada: Satan Exposed* (Cascade Books, an imprint of Wipf and Stock Publishers, 2011), Kindle edition, 5. Tripp also has a great blog called *The Amish Jihadist*. Exactly. How can you not love a blog with that name?

151 Elie Wiesel, *Night* (New York: Hill and Wang, 2006), 65. *Night* is a classic for a reason.

152 Ecclesiastes 4:9-12.

153 "Is The Human Hand Our Best Technology?" NPR TED Radio Hour, February 26, 2013, http://www.npr.org/templates/transcript/transcript.php?storyId=173002916.

154 Agassi, *Open*, 251.

155 Luke 24:47.

156 Romans 6.

157 In listening to Jay-Z's latest album, I realized that there is an amazing lyrical power about rising and a complete lack of acknowledgement of God's part in it. I think that's where God takes a backseat to pride. Jay-Z, Magna Carta... *Holy Grail*, Roc-A-Fella, Roc Nation, Universal, July 4, 2013.

breakfast.

158 John 21.

waves, vectors, and you.

159 Matthew 26.

160 Luke 19.

161 Mathew 19.

162 Matthew 23. Read it—it has some real zingers.

163 Mark 2.

164 Luke 15:11-32.

165 2 Kings 5.

166 "Kathryn Schulz: Don't regret regret." Filmed November 2011. TED video. Posted December 2011. http://www.ted.com/talks/kathryn_schulz_don_t_regret_regret.html. Here's another great TED Talk that everyone should listen to.

167 Brown, *Daring Greatly*, 92.

168 Rita Pierson is a champion of the human race. "What Role Do Relationships Play In Learning?" NPR TED Radio Hour, April 29, 2013, http://www.npr.org/templates/transcript/transcript.php?storyId=179822992.

169 One of my favorite books for marriage advice that is constantly saying, in a variety of ways, that it's who we are, not what we do, that will help a marriage the most. John M. Gottman, *The Seven Principles for Making Marriage Work: A Practical Guide from the Country's Foremost Relationship Expert* (Harmony, 2000).

170 John 1:12.

171 Romans 5:1.

172 Romans 8:1; Colossians 2:14-16.

173 Ephesians 1:4.

174 Romans 8:35-39.

175 Ephesians 2:10.

176 Romans 14:17.

177 So many books speak of getting to that point: entirely occupied with the good that the bad fades but this one is the latest to hit me over the head. Johnston, *The Cloud of Unknowing.*

gazelles.

178 For the record, I don't know anyone in M83, nor do I get any kind of royalty from you buying their song. But I have played them in church more than any other band because their music is so good. The band is led by Anthony Gonzalez, and if I ever get the chance to meet him, I will thank him for speaking to me in a way that no other bands do. M83, *Hurry Up, We're Dreaming*, Naïve/Mute, October 18, 2011.

Some final thanks.

Heidi: There are a million things, but thanks for making me stop that other book I was writing and write this one. It really was your idea Promise.

Whitney and Jordan: Seriously, that conversation in the foyer that day was all I needed. Thanks for that and all the ways you inspire me.

Branches: It's pretty cool that I get to "test out" all these ideas on you. You're the coolest group of guinea pigs the world has ever seen. But, seriously, you truly are an amazing, inspiring group of people who are everything a church should be. Thanks for all you do!

Ben: There aren't many people who do stuff as fast as I like them to do stuff and you are one of them. And you care. You're an amazing friend. Thanks for all the filming, editing, feedback, criticisms, and encouragement.

Bryan: Thanks for the editing. You kicked some butt and were a joy to work with in every way. You had your first baby right in the middle of this thing and it didn't slow down. Not at all. You're awesome! If there are any errors, it's because I messed with it after you were done. Can't wait to work together on the next book.

A couple of friends and family: You were Kickstarter supporters, but you were way more than that, too. Your financial gifts were beyond what I would have ever imagined, and I can't thank you enough—not just for helping to pay for this, but for the trust that those kind of gifts mean. You're generous and creative people who are changing our city and this world. Keep it up!

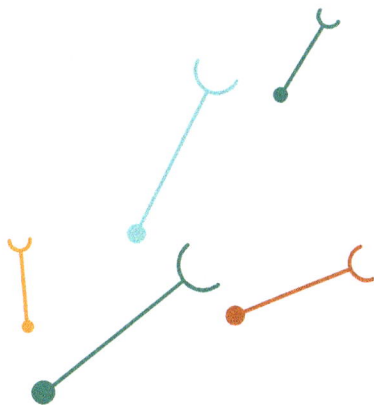

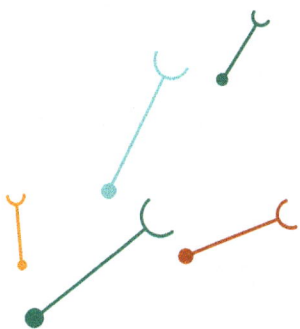

www.ingramcontent.com/pod-product-compliance
Lightning Source LLC
Chambersburg PA
CBHW060654150426
42813CB00053B/810